Friends from Beyond the Veil

Friends from Beyond the Veil

Compiled by
Shirley Bahlmann

CFI
Springville, Utah

ISBN 13: 978-1-55517-989-2

Published by CFI, an imprint of Cedar Fort, Inc.
2373 W. 700 S., Springville, UT, 84663
Distributed by Cedar Fort, Inc., www.cedarfort.com

LIBRARY OF CONGRESS CATALOGING-IN-PUBLICATION DATA
Friends beyond the veil : firsthand accounts of interactions with the supernatural / compiled by Shirley Bahlmann.
p. cm.
ISBN-13: 978-1-55517-989-2
1. Supernatural. 2. Occultism. 3. Spirits. I. Bahlmann, Shirley. II. Title.

BF1439.F75 2007
133.9--dc22

2006033394

Cover design by Nicole Williams
Cover design © 2007 by Lyle Mortimer
Edited by Kammi Rencher
Typeset by Kammi Rencher

Printed in the United States of America

10 9 8 7 6 5 4 3 2 1

Printed on acid-free paper

Dedication

This one's for Carolyn Bessey and Jackie Brown, two of the most mysterious librarians I've ever encountered.

Disclaimer

This book was created from personal interviews I conducted over the course of several months. I make no claims that the experiences I've compiled are either true or false.

Although this book warns against inviting evil spirits into your life, many of the stories tell of friendly, loving spirits who only want to help, and other spirits who seem to be merely curious.

These stories were told to me by people who claimed to actually see, hear, or feel the spirits around them. I simply wrote them down. Take them as you will.

Table of Contents

Preface

This book came about by accident. I never planned to write a collection of spirit or "ghost" stories—I don't even like scary movies.

It all began when I was researching pioneer stories and came across several 1800s accounts of angelic visitations and ghostly appearances. I found enough that I decided to write a book of pioneer ghost stories. The next thing I knew, someone told me about an old doctor's house that had done dual duty as a medical office at the turn of the twentieth century. Tales of a face seen in the turret window, even when the house was empty, made it seem a perfect candidate for my project.

Intrigued, I interviewed people who'd lived there, hoping to glean another pioneer-era ghost story. Instead, I uncovered firsthand accounts of what appeared to be supernatural forces at work. These modern-day experiences wouldn't fit in with my pioneer book, so I had to set the story aside.

Then more stories of modern-day supernatural sightings followed, with individuals telling me about seeing, hearing, or feeling spirits around them. Some stories were comforting, some were not. By the time I'd gathered nearly a dozen experiences, I got an uncomfortable feeling, like some invisible entity was looking over my shoulder.

What was I doing? Was I simply amassing a collection of tales that had no purpose except to titillate ghoulish imaginations? Was I creating a growing book of sensational stories with no redeeming value? A couple of family members added to my doubts when they cautioned me about delving into stories of hauntings, since that mindset could most certainly invite scary things in to visit me. I thought about abandoning the project altogether.

Then I spoke to an extraordinary person named Ranae Lee, who took the time to explain her point of view on five different types of spirits.

Suddenly, this book felt right. It was as though it had metamorphosed into a tool that could help mortals identify the different types of spirits. I finally felt like this information could be of help to readers who'd like to know whether the spirits they encounter are there for good or bad reasons.

As this book grew story by story, it was interesting to realize that some people seem able to brush more closely against the world of spirits than others. In some cases, this heightened sensitivity may be explained by a near-death experience. In other cases, it seemed that the individual has had the ability since childhood.

There is a section in this book of stories about evil spirits. From this rose some debate among the book's contributors about the role of ouija boards and palm reading. One contributor believes that a ouija board is simply a piece of inanimate wood that can't harbor evil. People manipulate the arrow to point out the letters for what they want it to say. The intent of the user draws in whatever experience may follow.

Someone else disagreed, saying that the main way a ouija board works is through spiritual intervention. "You can manipulate it, yeah, but just having it there creates an entry for spirits if they want to take it."

Another person said, "If talking about spirits invites

them in, then ouija boards and séances and stuff like that do the same thing."

Other debates arose from this section of the book. One of the stories in this collection carries a warning against palm reading. Yet one person expressed the opinion that it depended on who was doing it. If an evil person were to read your palm, it would be a different matter than opening the contours of your hand to a trusted friend.

And then there is the biggest debate of all: do ghosts even exist? Some people believe that every story must have a logical explanation, such as in the case of Jeanette Branham.

When Jeannette was three years old, she couldn't seem to go through a frigid winter night in her little bed snuggled up against the wall without kicking her covers off. Her parents tried tucking the blanket edges under the mattress, but it did no good. They became so frustrated that they started checking on her throughout the night.

One time, her father went into her room and noticed that his little daughter had kicked off her blankets yet again, with the bulk of them out of sight between the bed and the wall. Dad reached over, took hold of the short end of the covers, and gave a tug.

They didn't budge. It was as though some unseen entity had hold of the other end and refused to let go. Confused, Dad gave another hard pull. The unseen force on the far side of the bed still refused to relinquish the warm blankets.

A chill ran down Dad's back as he stared at the empty place where the blankets held fast. What strange force was at work here?

His resolve strengthened by sudden fear, Dad grabbed the balky fabric in both fists and yanked for all he was worth. The cover tore free and Dad staggered backward, the edge of the blanket scattering icy bits of frost on Jeannette's nightgown as it sailed over her.

It turned out that the poorly insulated wall beside Jeannette's bed conducted the cold from outside to the inside, which froze the blanket to the wall in stages, gradually pulling it off the bed in small degrees throughout the night until Jeannette was left out in the cold.

These are not the kind of stories this book is made of. Not unless you can come up with some earthly explanation for the lightning that raged through the bottom floor of a house one night for hours. Or for the time when someone moved furniture and walked around upstairs when the women who heard it knew no one else was home? Who . . . or what . . . grabbed the teenage boy in the deserted yard and threw him into the garage door? What made the straw doll fly toward the strange girl who was looking for a place to stay?

All but a couple of the stories in this volume were written from firsthand accounts, the people I spoke with claiming to have seen, heard, or felt some very strange things. A few are written from accounts given by family members, if the original participants weren't able to speak to me. Some have asked that their names be changed and their hometowns left unidentified. I honored their requests.

The people whose stories are found in this book swear that what they saw and heard was real. I leave it to you, the reader, to decide what to believe.

Acknowledgments

A big thanks and a bright nightlight for my proofreaders: Bob Bahlmann, Val Sorensen, Judi Hansen, Jeanette Branham, Jackie Brown, and Larry and Gayelene Henrickson. Thanks to Clair Erickson for helping me track some things down, and to Matt Twilley and author Linda Paulson Adams for their title suggestions.

And thanks to all those who were willing to tell their stories to me.

Introduction

Identifying Ghosts

Information in this chapter is from an interview with Ranae Lee, and expresses her personal opinions and experiences.

As you will find from reading these stories, not all ghosts are alike.

Ranae Lee said she's survived three near-death episodes (NDE), an experience which, no matter how brief, seems to heighten one's sensitivity to spirits.

Lee described her spiritual gift as "weird, because it kind of catches me off guard sometimes." She once saw a sobbing four-year-old running from a house toward her moving car. She can't always tell at first if what she sees is a ghost, so she was afraid she might hit him. By the time she realized the crying child was a spirit, she was quite shaken up.

Now she can tell what kind of spirit she sees right from the start. There are several kinds of spirits, and Lee likes to group them into five general categories.

The first kind of haunting is made up of spirits whose families mourn them to the point that they stay in an effort to comfort loved ones left behind. In many cases, this involves a child. Sometimes, after the rest of the family dies and moves on, the lost spirit feels unsure of what to do.

As a case in point, Lee once toured a bed and breakfast establishment that was for sale. In one of the rooms, she sensed an unseen presence. She turned to the owner and asked, "Have you, by chance, had any problems with ghosts?"

The lady looked startled. "Yes, as a matter of fact." She pointed at two old sepia photos on the wall of two little ten-year-old girls, the images facing each other.

"Those are twin girls who used to live here," she said. "That picture on the left never stays on the wall. Just about every morning it's on the floor, but the other one is hung the very same way and it always stays put."

One of Lee's strongest claims is that of clairaudient communication, which is the ability to hear and talk with spirits in her mind. So Lee "spoke" to the spirit, and found a bewildered young teenage girl, born in the mid 1800s. She'd contracted a fatal case of pneumonia at about age twelve, and her family grieved for her to the point that she stayed around. She got stuck and she was mad about it.

"Wouldn't you like to be done with this?" Lee asked her. "Just pray to Heavenly Father and ask the Lord to send those who could help you."

After a short time, the ghost left. A few minutes later she came back, vibrant and glowing with joy. She was excited to have found her way to the other side.

Another category of earthbound spirits consists of those who've gone through a traumatic experience. They may get so wrapped up in the emotion of that moment that they stay around to try and remedy the situation. Sometimes they keep trying for years to fix what went wrong.

Lee reported an experience with her slightly handicapped Uncle Pete, who'd drowned. A few years after his death, Lee had a visit from another deceased relative of hers, asking if Lee could get Uncle Pete to listen. It seems that Uncle Pete's handicap stayed with him after death, and his spirit was so terrified that he wouldn't let anyone near. Any time a helpful spirit approached, he'd panic and cover his head with his arms. Not wanting to force their help, the kindly spirits would retreat.

With patience, Lee was able to convince Uncle Pete that the spirits around him wanted to help. He finally let them near enough to give him some guidance. Later, he came back to visit Lee. His handicap was gone, and he was joyful and strong.

Lee says that the Lord loves everyone, even the spirits who have trapped themselves on earth. He wants them to progress, but he won't force them. "It's so much better over there that I can't imagine why anyone would want to hang out over here," Lee says.

A third kind of ghost is one who is tied to earthly things, choosing to remain close to what was important to him or her in mortal life.

In the book Return From Tomorrow by George Ritchie, the author reports of seeing spirits go through the motions of their earthly jobs. That was their god on earth, so they're still doing it. In these cases, the spirit's "god" can be a job or a car or any other earthly object or pursuit.

Many other spirits like to stay in one spot. They think it's their place, and may not even realize that they're dead.

Lee says that sometimes there's a learning process that has to go on with those who are trapped on earth, and it doesn't take place immediately. Sometimes it takes a hundred years or more.

Lee and her family acquired a home built many years before by a prominent resident. On their first day in the house, they were in an upstairs bedroom. As soon as they conducted a special dedication prayer over the building, they heard a crash. Hurrying downstairs, they saw a chandelier spinning around in the room directly beneath the bedroom.

Lee got the impression that the previous owner was not happy they were there.

"He was benign but concerned about the house. I had a talk with him and told him that the Lord had sent us to this area, and everything belongs to the Lord anyway, so he just needed to get used to us."

A fourth kind of spiritual presence can come from ones sent to watch over or guard a home or an area, especially if it's been dedicated. Dedicating a place is essentially praying over it, and asking for God's spirit to dwell there.

"I've walked into a place where I've just felt the spirits the Lord sent very strongly. They very rarely let themselves be known because they're just doing their jobs," Lee says.

Some of the stories in this volume contain events where spirits appear to have interacted with family members before birth or after death. Those stories are also included in this category. [1]

The fifth category consists of evil spirits. Satan's host will worm their way through any opening or take advantage of every opportunity to torment people. They can masquerade as other beings, and tell lies.

Lee once observed a woman practice a questionable form of alternative health on another woman. A dark entity emerged from the patient and gave them riddles and rhymes for about an hour. In Lee's opinion, the woman should have immediately cast it away from their presence in the name of Jesus Christ.

"The adversary will look for any opportunity to get pity for him and his hosts so that he can get a foot in the door, so to speak," Lee said. "He'll play on people's compassion

1. "Sarah's Still Here" and "Fishing with Grandpa," suggest that spirits may "live" with their earthly families both before and after this life. This was also suggested by a niece of Teri Morris ("Lady on the Stairs") who related an incident of a couple whose dead daughter wanted them to know that she's still around her family. That account is not included in this book, because I wasn't able to speak to the girl's parents personally.

and make them think 'Oh, it's so sad, I feel sorry for them,' but people need to know the difference and understand when they're dealing with demons. They need to leave them alone."

Lee says that the evil ones will try to convince you that they want to repent. Some people urge them to go toward the light. This is a complete waste of time and is also spiritually dangerous. "People don't realize that they if they're dealing with an evil spirit, they can't tell it to go toward the light and move on to the next world," Lee said. "It won't do any good, and it could even harm you by giving it a chance to interact with you. If people are going to attempt interaction with spirits, they need to recognize whether it's Satan's hosts or someone who's become earthbound," Lee said.

Lee explained that people on earth have no stewardship over the evil ones or what happens to them, either those that followed Satan out of heaven or those who've lived on this earth and have chosen to join his ranks. Evil people are counted among Satan's host.

Some people make it easy for the evil spirits. They invite them in when they give up their agency and awareness through any kind of mind-altering drug use, including alcohol. Losing control of their mental faculties creates the perfect opportunity for evil spirits to enter. George Ritchie wrote in his book about seeing drunk people's auras "open up" and evil spirits dive in as soon as the unwitting hosts lost consciousness.

You can't help these evil spirits. They don't want your help. All they want is to hurt you in any way they can. They can have no power over you unless you allow it by inviting them in. Leave them completely alone.

According to Lee, one of the best ways to tell whether a spirit is innocent or evil is whether they're tormenting you or not. If they don't hurt you, then most likely they're just lost.

Just as benign spirits will generally hang around their earthly dwellings, evil spirits will take over houses if they can. They love to haunt houses, Lee says, but they can occupy land too.

"It seems that once evil takes over a place, it can be hard to get rid of," Lee says. "Have you ever walked into a place that just gives you the chills, like where the Mountain Meadow Massacre occurred, and you can feel the hair standing on the back of your neck? It's because the earth carries a memory. Sometimes the house itself can absorb that information and replay it over and over again."

This phenomenon is called Diallel Lines. Lee spent some time researching Diallel Lines with a physicist. Her studies led her to understand that Diallel Lines are similar to deoxyribonucleic acid, or DNA. DNA is the material inside the nucleus of cells that carries genetic information. In other words, it is the pattern or blueprint that makes things what they are.

Diallel Lines are a memory, or imprint, of things that have happened on the earth. Once in a while, when an event is intensely emotional, it can engrave Diallel Lines in the place where it happened. Then Diallel memory can replay the event again and again. That's why you might walk into a place and feel an immediate sense of unease, because the earth or a house carries a memory of something that happened there before. And if former events are replayed, then people may call the place "haunted."

Lee says of spirits, "They tend to go where they're invited, especially dark ones. One thing I have learned is that the minute you start talking about them, you can invite them quickly." She says that if you talk about your relatives, then they can be there with you immediately. Many spirits are assigned to watch over and help family members. Some people say that spirits are too busy to visit, but the spirit world has a totally different time frame. Most of the time, spirits come and go freely.

Spirits generally like to be able to communicate with somebody. When they find out that a person on earth has the ability to see or hear them, sometimes they bombard that person. Says Lee, "I've put up some rules, and they have to follow the rules."

Lee has come to find her spiritual gifts to be an amazing world to explore, but she also understands that she needs to be careful. She knows of one lady who is so wrapped up in her spiritual gifts that she's about to lose her family.

"It's so easy to get off balance and into a mode that you don't know how to juggle," said Lee. "Put your family and the Lord first, and the rest will fall into place."

Part 1
Angels and Family

Sarah's Still Here

No one else could have been responsible for saving the family's home.

"My daughter was killed eight years ago this week, on the 28th of February," Janie Van Komen said.

There were five teenagers in the car when it left the restaurant parking lot after breakfast. In a hurry to get to school before the bell rang, the young driver unwittingly pulled in front of an accelerating semi truck intent on taking the freeway on-ramp just beyond the restaurant's parking lot. There wasn't time for the trucker to stop, even though he locked his brakes in a desperate attempt to avoid a collision. The sound of squealing tires, shattering glass, and snapping metal mingled with the screams of onlookers.

One victim was rushed to a local medical facility, two were life-flighted to another hospital, and two ended up in the morgue.

Sarah Van Komen had just celebrated her birthday on February 3rd in her family's new home. Now she would be forever sixteen in their hearts.

"Over 2,000 people attended her viewing," Janie remembered. "Nearly that many tried to get into her funeral."

One of the funeral speakers, a respected church leader, surveyed the assembly from the pulpit. "He said that from the size of the crowd, Sarah must have had an impact on people's lives. He went on to predict that powerful things were about to take place."

Hearing these words, Janie wiped the tears from her eyes and glanced down the row at the solemn faces of her nine remaining children. Sarah's passing had left a painful gap in the family ranks. Janie wondered if the powerful things spoken of might be Sarah's influence to help her siblings make right choices. Janie thought that she'd never be able to truly recognize the impact Sarah had on their family until after she herself had died and could see her daughter again.

She was wrong.

"Sarah's been very active," Janie said. "One particular incident was very profound."

The Van Komen's new home was a brand new Fall 1996 Parade of Homes tour model. After Sarah's funeral, two of her sisters gathered up some of the hundreds of flowers that accompanied their sister's memorial service and carried them into their basement. In a labor of love, they painstakingly hung them upside down in rows that nearly covered the basement ceiling, then left them to dry. They planned, one day, to turn them into wreaths and flower arrangements.

Spring bloomed and ripened toward summer. The sisters' plans for Sarah's flowers were pushed into the background of their busy lives.

One warm day, Janie decided to turn on the central air conditioning system for the first time. It worked perfectly for a couple of days, but then for no apparent reason, it quit. Being the resourceful person that she is, Janie went into the basement and toyed with the controls, trying to figure out what was wrong.

"All of a sudden, the digital display just went completely wacko, flashing 9999 and 8888 and then everything went black," Janie said.

Deciding that this particular repair was beyond her abilities, Janie called on her husband, Bob, a general contractor, to see if he could figure it out. Bob soon discovered that one of the fuses in the electrical panel next to the furnace was missing. He checked the floor under the fuse box, and then looked all around the basement for the errant fuse, yet it was nowhere to be seen.

Figuring that one of the older children must have been messing around where they shouldn't, blown the fuse, then destroyed the evidence, Bob heaved a sigh and straightened up. He went out, got a replacement fuse, and put it in place. The air conditioning system hummed to life as soon as he turned it on, but moments later it shut itself off.

Scratching his head in puzzlement, Bob checked the owner's manual. Since the system was new to him, Bob figured he'd better brush up on the particulars. He followed the manual's instructions step by step. In one section, the meaning of a flashing green light was defined, followed by the meaning of the light flashing red. After following the steps and pushing the appropriate buttons, Bob was startled to see that the light was flashing both green and red. That particular situation wasn't covered anywhere in the manual.

Bob decided it was time to call in a specialist.

While the repairman worked on the system, Bob went in search of the fuse-stealing culprit. He started with his oldest child and worked his way down the ranks. Yet each one of his inquiries was met with blank stares.

"None of our kids even knew what he was taking about," Janie said. In fact, from the probing questions and vague answers that passed between parent and each child, it was evident that the children all mistakenly thought their father was referring to the electrical box.

"They were totally clueless," Janie said. "You can tell when kids are lying or fudging the truth. Even though Bob reassured them that he wasn't trying to accuse anyone or get them in trouble, that he just wanted to know what happened to the missing fuse, he didn't get anywhere. Not one of our kids even knew that there was a fuse in that box." Not only that, the fuse box was secured by a metal clip. Someone would have to know to lift the clip before they could take a fuse out.

It took the repairman all afternoon to discover that the safety device in the furnace had gone haywire. "He said it was one of the most unusual things he'd ever worked on," Janie said.

Apparently, the heating/cooling system was originally built to automatically shut off the gas supply if something went wrong. This feature would keep the unit from shooting out bursts of fire. But the safety system was defective.

"The repairman told us that whoever took that fuse out kept our house from burning down," Janie said. "With all the dried flowers hanging around the ceiling down there, it was a tinderbox."

When Bob heard the diagnosis, he turned to Janie and said, "There's only one explanation for this." Janie and Bob had the strong feeling that only Sarah could have been the one to pull the fuse out and keep their family safe.

Another thing attributed to Sarah's labors from the spirit world are Janie's many requests to speak. Over the past eight years, Janie has filled more than three hundred speaking engagements. Of a recent event, where Janie addressed young women who'd lost one of their group to a sudden bout of meningitis that made her sick on Thursday and took her life by the week's end, she said, "One thing I thought about is how God places his chess pieces way in advance. They had arranged for me to speak three months earlier. How could it be a coincidence that I would speak the very night when all those girls were struggling with the situation? It was like I was a kindred spirit, and they could all cry on my shoulder when they needed someone. And God set that up three months in advance."

Janie has actually wondered how some of the people who ask her to speak have even found her. One lady said it took her six months to finally get in touch. Perhaps Sarah helped her out. "It's part of the fulfillment of what I feel now was prophecy," Janie said. "There's a sketch of Sarah with the Savior, done by Jean Keaton. I get letters all the time from people whose lives have been impacted by that picture."

A few days after Sarah's funeral, her older sister, Rachel, went with Janie to hear a talk by author Blaine Yorgason in Syracuse, Utah. Yorgason and his wife, Kathy, had adopted an infant daughter named Charity who lived several years beyond all medical expectations. She'd finally died just before her eighth birthday. Yorgason ended his talk by relating an experience when he heard Charity's spirit say "Hi, Daddy."

Touched by his message, Janie and Rachel waited for the crowd around Yorgason to diminish before approaching him to introduce themselves. Before they could catch his attention, he turned away and began gathering his things. When the Van Komens got close to him, he paused, as if sensing their presence.

"It was the most amazing experience," Janie said. "As we entered his space all three of us began to weep. There was some kind of power surrounding us." Yorgason turned and put out his hand. No one could say anything as Yorgason clasped Janie's hand in both of his. Janie regained her composure and apologized, explaining that she was still emotional from the death of her daughter earlier in the week.

"I know," Yorgason said. "I didn't know it was your daughter that it happened to, but I know." He patted Janie's hand. "Would you like to know what happened after Charity spoke to me?" Janie and Rachel nodded.

Yorgason said that after Charity died, his other daughter was very concerned. She wanted to know if Charity just floated around doing good deeds or if she had some kind of house or home base. Every time the family got together, she'd bring up the subject to the point that her brothers would roll their eyes in exasperation.

Several weeks later, Yorgason felt Charity's presence again while he was praying. Immediately, his other daughter's concerns came to his mind. Almost fearfully, he posed her question to the Lord.

Instead of a feeling of chastisement, however, he was instantly flooded with a sense of peace. Then, very clearly, these words formed in his mind, "Daddy, I have been sealed to you and Mom by a servant of the Living God. You will always be my family, and I will always be your daughter. Your home will always be my home, and until you join me here, I will dwell in your home with you."

When Yorgason fell silent, Janie was flooded with instant warmth. "Oh, my gosh," she said. "I already know that what you're saying is true."

Janie's mind flew back to a time when Sarah was barely two years old. Since Janie's husband was a general contractor, the family had built and sold houses repeatedly before moving to West Point, Utah. Sarah was a clingy toddler, a real Mama's girl, until a nice older lady came to visit. She'd no sooner settled herself on the sofa when Sarah climbed up beside her and snuggled into her side. After a moment, she climbed up onto the lady's lap. Then she reached up and looked into the woman's ears, patted her cheeks, and even looked down her blouse with the innocent curiosity of a toddler.

"She was crawling all over the woman," Janie said. "It embarrassed me. But the woman was older and loved it."

Janie worried that maybe Sarah wasn't getting enough attention, so after the woman left, Janie took Sarah into her arms and stroked her long, black hair. "Sarah, I love you so much," she murmured.

Sarah looked up at her mother. "I love you, too, Mama, and I love that other grandma."

Janie said, "There's something about our mortal bodies that keeps us from spirit-to-spirit communication. I had to ask Sarah, 'What other grandma?'"

"You know, Mama, the other grandma who used to live with us in all the other houses.'"

Janie stopped cold. Her visitor did have a slight resemblance to her grandmother, who used to spend the night at Janie's house whenever she made her regular visits to Salt Lake City for chemotherapy treatments. But that was before Sarah was born.

"We had been counseled by a church leader that Sarah would always be a part of our family," Janie said. "And that we should not offend her by leaving her out."

And Sarah wasn't about to let anyone forget it.

Fishing with Grandpa

Little Ginny already knew her deceased grandfather.

According to her mother, Dionne, Ginny's a spitfire. Not only that, she seems to have an open channel from the mortal to the spirit world. At least, she did when she was younger.

One day, Ginny pranced into the living room where her mother was doing some paperwork.

"Grandpa used to take me fishing," Ginny announced, plopping tummy first on the couch cushions beside her mother.

Startled, her mother looked down at the blonde head and asked, "What?"

"Grandpa took me fishing."

"When?"

Ginny bounced up and down softly before she answered, "Just a little while ago."

Her mother sat quietly for a moment in her uncertainty. Finally, she said, "But Grandpa's not here anymore."

"I was fishing with him before," Ginny insisted, boosting herself up to sit beside her mom.

"We'd never been fishing," Dionne said. "We didn't fish." But she decided to play along. "How do you fish?" she asked her daughter.

"You go to the cabin, you go to the lake, then you put

your pole over the water," Ginny said earnestly, swinging her little arms out in front of her, one fist above the other as though hanging on to a long, slender rod. "Your string goes in, then you're fishing." She dropped her hands in her lap and gazed at her mother with satisfaction. There was no doubt in her wide blue eyes.

Before he died, Dionne's father had been an avid fisherman.

Dionne decided to settle the matter once and for all. She stood up and pulled out the family photo album. "Is the grandpa you went fishing with in here?" she asked, settling in beside her daughter and turning the pages slowly.

As soon as the book fell open to a photograph of Dionne's father, Ginny planted her finger on his chin. "There he is!"

Dionne stared at the image. "Are you sure?" she whispered.

"Yes, Grandpa, this man," Ginny said, nodding happily.

"My dad died in 1983," Dionne said. "And Ginny wasn't born until two years later, in 1985."

Dancing down the Hall

Krystal couldn't understand why she wasn't allowed to visit Grandma anymore.

Krystal got out of the car and ran ahead of her mother. She jumped up on Grandma's porch and banged her fist against the door before pushing it open. "Grandma, I'm here!"

"Is that my Krystal-Queen?" Grandma's voice called from the other room.

"Yes, I am!" Krystal answered, running to where her grandmother sat in her padded rocker, an oxygen canella stretched across her upper lip.

At first, Krystal had fretted over the unfamiliar tube under Grandma's nose, but then Grandma had let her try it on. Krystal was comforted when she discovered that gentle puffs of air came out of the little holes to help her grandma feel better.

The canella had appeared shortly after Krystal's mother said she was getting too big to sit on Grandma's lap. That decree bothered Krystal, because she loved Grandma's lap, Grandma's house, Grandma's hugs, Grandma's everything. She was safe with Grandma. Krystal thought home was all right too, but it wasn't the same. Mom made her do chores, and Mom was always busy. Krystal didn't like school much at all, where some kids called her retarded and mimicked her. She loved Grandma's house the best. Grandma didn't care how tall Krystal grew or if she didn't act like everyone else. Krystal was Grandma's perfect princess.

"Go get your crown," Grandma said.

Krystal ran into the extra bedroom where Grandma kept a small assortment of tiaras. Krystal passed over the painted silver crown encrusted with pink plastic stones and picked up a rhinestone tiara instead. She set it carefully on her head and walked with uncharacteristic slowness into the bathroom so she could see herself in the mirror. She turned her head one way and then another, delighted as the sparkly stones winked back at her. She pulled her hair up on top of her head, letting it spill down like a waterfall on either side of her face. She liked how it looked, but didn't know how to make it stay.

Krystal hurried back into the living room where her mother sat beside Grandma, saying something about pills. Krystal waited, impatient but quiet, until her mother finished talking.

"Grandma, please make my hair pretty," she begged.

"It's already pretty."

"No, fancy pretty."

"All right," Grandma said. "Go get the pins and a comb, then sit on the floor in front of me."

Krystal hurried to get the pins. She knew right where they were. She scooped up a comb and hurried back to Grandma. Soon she was seated in front of Grandma's knees, her eyes closed in bliss as Grandma combed through her hair, working out the knots with gentle fingers, pinning the locks up with care. The murmur of Grandma and Mom's voices nearly put Krystal to sleep.

When Grandma finished, Krystal replaced the comb and stared at her reflection in the mirror. She clapped her hands in delight and rushed back to Grandma. "Thank you, Grandma! I love you!" She bent over, wrapped her arms around Grandma, and squeezed.

Grandma winced. "You're welcome, Princess."

"Krystal, not so hard," Mom said sharply.

Krystal pulled back, confusion in her eyes.

"It's fine, Krystal," Grandma said. "You can hug me softly, all right?"

Krystal smiled and twirled in a circle. "Dance with me, Grandma!" She held her hands out, but Grandma didn't take them. They used to dance together all the time, but lately, Grandma hadn't wanted to dance at all.

"Krystal, I'd love to dance with you, but I'm just too tired right now. You dance for me, okay? Turn the radio on. I'll watch and clap for you."

"Okay." Krystal swayed over to the radio and punched the buttons. She danced until she was dizzy, and Grandma clapped after every song.

At last it was time to go. Krystal walked over to hug Grandma good-bye. She remembered to hug her softly. When she pulled away, she looked into Grandma's tired face. Even though Grandma smiled, Krystal could see the fatigue behind her eyes.

Suddenly, Krystal lifted the tiara from her head, turned it around in her clumsy fingers, and set it on Grandma's gray hair.

"There," said Krystal, stepping back and giving her Grandma a big grin. "I'm the princess, you're the queen."

Grandma laughed. "Krystal, you're so good for me."

"'Bye, Grandma. See you later!" and Krystal ran out the door to the car.

The next day, Krystal sat at her desk in school, staring out the window and waiting for the dismissal bell. When she heard the classroom door open, she turned to see who it was. She was puzzled to see her mother walk into the room. It wasn't time for school to be done yet. Krystal waved, but her mother didn't seem to notice. Mom's eyes were red, like she'd been crying. Krystal watched with worry as her mother whispered something to the teacher. Then she walked over to Krystal's desk. "Come on, Krystal, we're going home."

As soon as they were in the hall, Krystal said, "Let's go to Grandma's."

Mom put her hand over her mouth and gave a strange sound like a cough. She wiped her eyes, then said, "We can't go to Grandma's anymore, Krystal, because Grandma died."

"But I want to see Grandma," Krystal insisted.

Mom shook her head. "We can't, Krystal, she's gone."

"Gone where?"

"I know it's hard for you to understand, but Grandma's dead. We can't go see her."

Krystal moved toward the car on leaden legs. She didn't understand. She knew Grandma loved her; she knew Grandma wanted to see her. She didn't know why Mom wouldn't take her to Grandma's house.

Krystal didn't go to school the next day. She didn't go to Grandma's house either, even though she asked Mom to take her several times. Finally, Mom got impatient. "Oh, Krystal, how can I make you understand?"

Krystal hung her head, tears of disappointment trembling on her lashes.

Mom went to her room and came back with a plastic bag. She handed it to Krystal and murmured, "Here. It's a present from Grandma."

Excited, Krystal opened the bag. All the tiaras from Grandma's house crowded together in the bottom of the bag. Krystal looked up at her mother, her face stricken with betrayal. "You saw Grandma without me!" she cried.

"Krystal, I didn't see Grandma," Mom said. "I just went to her house, but Grandma's not there anymore. She's gone to heaven."

"Take me to heaven," Krystal begged. "I have to give these back to Grandma. She said never to bring them home. I can only play with them at her house for a special privilege. It's not a special privilege here. Only at Grandma's."

Mom sighed. "I'm sorry, Krystal. I thought the crowns

would make you feel better. I'll take them if you want me to."

"No!" Krystal pressed the sack to her chest and ran. She dashed into her room and shut the door behind her. She plopped down on her bed, the bag of tiaras clutched tightly on her lap. She rocked back and forth, back and forth, wondering what she could do to make things right.

Then she had an idea. Sometimes Mom called Grandma on the telephone and let Krystal talk, too. Krystal opened her door and looked out into the hall. No one was there. She made her way to the telephone and picked up the receiver. She pushed some numbers, but it didn't work. She tried some different numbers, but she still couldn't get Grandma to answer.

"Krystal," her mother called. "Are you playing with the phone?"

"No!" Krystal said. She wasn't playing. She was calling Grandma, but she didn't know the right numbers. She hung up the phone and walked back to her room to think some more.

Maybe she could walk to Grandma's house since Mom wouldn't drive her. But she didn't know the way. She all but strangled the bag in her tight fists. "Grandma, where are you?" she whispered. But there was no answer.

The next day, Mom told Krystal to put on a dress for Grandma's funeral. At the mention of Grandma's name, Krystal rushed so fast to dress that she ended up with one black and one blue sock on. She didn't care. She hurried out to sit in the car, the bag of tiaras resting on her lap. Her mother didn't see any harm in Krystal taking them to the funeral, so she didn't say anything when she got in and started the car.

As soon as they arrived at the chapel, Krystal dashed out of the car and ran inside. Mom caught up to her and led her into a room where a big wooden box sat up on legs. Krystal looked into the box. It had soft white cloth all around inside, and there was a lady asleep in there, her head resting on a puffy pillow. It looked like a nice place to sleep. The lady in the box looked a little bit like Grandma, but Krystal was unmoved. "Where's Grandma?" she asked.

Mom pointed into the box. "She's right there."

Krystal shook her head. "Where's Grandma?"

"Grandma died, Krystal. That's all that is left of her."

"No! Where's my real Grandma?"

Eventually, Mom had to take an unsatisfied Krystal into the chapel for the funeral service. The double doors were open into the empty hallway. Krystal fingered the tiaras through the plastic bag and stared out into the hallway, paying no attention to the speakers. Her mother didn't try to redirect her attention, grateful that Krystal was quiet.

Just as the final song began, Krystal let go of her strangle hold on the tiara bag and began clapping with unbounded enthusiasm. Her mother reached over and grabbed her hands. "No, Krystal, we don't clap."

"I found Grandma!" Krystal said, bouncing up and down in her seat, not bothering to keep her voice down.

Relieved that Krystal had finally come to terms with her grandmother's death, Mom cast a glance at the closed casket sitting at the front of the room. "Yes, Krystal, Grandma's at peace."

"No," Krystal said, shaking her head, her delighted gaze fixed through the open doors. She pointed down the hallway. "There she is! See? Grandma's all better! She's dancing down the hall! She said I can keep the crowns until I see her again, because now I'm her special privilege for always."

The Rose Globe

Grandma didn't want anything to do with turning ninety years old. She got her wish.

When her husband, Seldon, died in 1973, sixty-three-year-old Geneva announced that she refused to ever reach ninety years old. "She also said that if Dad wasn't there to greet her when she passed on, she'd be coming back," her daughter, Naomi, said.

Naomi's daughter, Deanna, added, "Grandma wondered why she had to live without Grandpa for so long. She always thought that maybe she wasn't worthy enough to die."

"When she was eighty-nine, she couldn't see or eat very well," Naomi said, "And when she fell two weeks before she died, she just went downhill."

Geneva cut it pretty close, dying on April 1, 2000, three days short of her ninetieth birthday.

"I was really close to Grandma, so it was hard for me, especially because I wasn't there when she died," Deanna said. "I didn't get a chance to say good-bye."

Naomi, a cosmetologist, made arrangements to fix her mother's hair as a last act of loving service. She took Deanna and her other daughter, Joyce, with her to the funeral home on the evening of April 2nd.

As Naomi combed and styled Geneva's hair, Deanna applied makeup to her grandmother's face. They dressed her, and then the mortician wheeled Grandma's body into the viewing room, where he left the descendants alone.

"We sat there and visited with her for a minute, and talked to her," Naomi said. "Then we stood in a circle and hugged."

"Joyce and I used to have feuds," Deanna said, "but the experience of getting Grandma ready for burial really did something to us that day and brought us closer together."

"Just as we were ready to leave, one of the girls said, 'See you later, alligator,'" Naomi said. "I replied, 'After awhile, crocodile,' because that's what Gram always said to the girls."

"When we got home, I asked if Joyce and Mom thought that Gram noticed what we did," Deanna said. "Joyce wondered if Grandma realized how much we cared. Then she asked, 'Do you think she knew we were there?'"

"All of a sudden, I heard a *swish*," Naomi said. "Joyce was closest to the rose globe on the table, and I said, 'What was that, Joyce?'"

A rose globe is a round hollow glass ball with a hole in the bottom. Its purpose is to display flowers in a water filled environment, sealed with a rubber stopper.

"I don't know," Joyce said.

"Then a *swish, whoosh,* sound came, and all of a sudden there was water dripping on the floor," Deanna said.

"I walked closer to the table and there was water all over," Naomi said. "I looked at the empty rose globe, then picked it up. The seal was tight. There was no leak in it anywhere. It scared the girls."

"Joyce was freaked out," Deanna said. "She was one of those types that thought that kind of stuff would never happen."

Naomi reassured her girls. "It's Grandma. She's letting us know that she appreciates what we just did for her, and that she's all right."

The next day, Naomi went to the flower shop to order flowers. The florist happened to be the one who'd sold them their rose globe. "Have you ever had anyone mention a rose globe leaking?" Naomi asked.

"No."

"I had one leak last night, but the seal wasn't broken."

"No way!" the florist said, staring at Naomi in disbelief.

"There were no cracks or holes or anything."

"I've never heard of such a thing."

Naomi told the florist that she thought her mother was behind it. After a moment of thought, the florist said, "That's how I'd put it too."

Deanna has the rose globe now, and she uses it all the time. She changes the flowers and the water and seals the globe with the rubber stopper, just like it was sealed on the day the water mysteriously gushed out of it. But it's never leaked, not one drop, since the day after Grandma died.

Geneva was buried on April 4, which would have been her ninetieth birthday. "We let ninety helium balloons go at the cemetery," Naomi said. "Mom didn't want to hear ninety, be ninety, or have anything to do with ninety years old. Since she died on April Fools' Day, it was almost like she was saying, 'I told you, I told you, I wouldn't be ninety!'"

Peaceful Spirits

Loved ones are watching over us.

Waking up in the middle of the night was not unusual for Teri Rodeman. If the symptoms of diabetes or non-Hodgkins lymphoma cancer didn't wake her, then the painful bone spurs that prodded a nearly constant ache to march up and down her spine would.

Teri had never had back trouble until after her three-year stint as a Certified Nurse Assistant at a Long Beach, California, hospital in the 1970s. Struggling to assist patients who were heavier than she was weakened her back.

In an effort to alleviate her symptoms, the war office put her in a medical collar and sent her to work as a war secretary. She stayed on the job until they refused to give her time off for a honeymoon. Teri quit her job to get married. Twenty-three years later, she was disheartened to receive the diagnosis of cancer in her already weakened body.

One dark morning in July of 2003, Teri woke up in her mobile home in Benton City, Washington. It was about 3 o'clock. Teri realized that she wasn't in any particular pain, so what had woken her?

Then she noticed a subtle light in her room that had gently penetrated her sleep. When Teri focused on the source of light, she became aware of several gossamer silhouettes hovering over her bed. Although they didn't shine forth actual beams of light, the human figures that looked down on her and her sleeping husband, Bob, radiated a soft inner glow.

Teri stared, transfixed, at the nearly transparent images. Although she couldn't quite make out their features, she got the distinct impression that one of them was male and three were female. As she gazed up at them in wonder, she realized that the man was her father, who had died a few years earlier. Two of the beings were her aunts, and the other female was her cousin.

As she moved her eyes from figure to figure, Teri was amazed to see that the Nottingham lace tablecloth hanging on the wall opposite her bed undulated in gentle movements from side to side, as though in the path of a mild breeze. Yet the window was closed. Teri soon realized that it was the visiting beings hovering between her and the lace that made it appear to move. Their transparent energy pulsed in soft waves, creating the illusion of movement.

The curtains that covered the closed window off to her right also seemed to be moving in the same non-existent breeze, because one of the spirits watched her from a spot just in front of the window.

Teri felt a sense of love and deep caring emanating from her nocturnal visitors. After gazing on the peaceful spirits for a good quarter of an hour, Teri fell back into a light, peaceful sleep. When she woke up two hours later, her visitors were gone.

The same beings have come to see Teri a couple of times since. "I don't know for sure why I have these nocturnal visits," Teri said.

The most recent reported visit was on January 20, 2005. They hovered for an hour before leaving at around 6:15 AM Even though Bob got up at 6 o'clock, he didn't see them.

Perhaps Teri's chronic pain makes her more sensitive to the spirit world. Perhaps it's because they're her family that she is privileged to know they are watching over her.

Most people who find themselves living in a haunted house only want to get the spirits out of there. But Teri feels just the opposite.

"I get the feeling that they're protecting us somehow," Teri said. "I'm very grateful for them."

The Rocking Chair

Is it intense family love and loyalty that keeps the old chair rocking?

Jennie Hansen's pioneer ancestors made one of the first pieces of furniture in the Salt Lake Valley after they relocated there in the mid-1800s. The hand carved rocking chair is completely handmade. Even the wooden bolts that hold the pieces of the rocker together were hand carved by Jennie's great-great grandfather, in a labor of love for his wife, who had two little children and nothing to use to comfortably nurse the baby.

One can only guess at the countless hours Jennie's great-great grandmother spent rocking fussy little ones to sleep or soothing squabbles or just using the chair to help her recuperate from the rigors of a busy day. Whatever it was, it seems that some kind of intense nurturing energy, combined with the selfless love that built the rocker, accompanies the chair to this day.

The family story goes that when great-great-grandma eventually died, her daughter inherited the rocking chair. That night, the chair began to rock back and forth, back and forth, of its own accord.

Then, when Jennie's great-grandmother died, again, it rocked by itself as the next owner watched.

"The story is that in every generation, either the daughter or granddaughter of the woman who died saw the chair rock," Jennie said. "Whenever the person who owned the chair passed away, the person who inherited the chair would see it rocking as gently as a mother rocks her baby, but I can only give you personal insight on my own and my mother's stories."

Hansen's mother lost the love and guidance of her own mother when she was just ten years old. The aunts wouldn't let the little girl into the sick room to see her mother during her final illness, so she was left alone on the enclosed porch to deal with her grief in solitude.

The old family rocking chair was on the porch, too. Without any preamble, the old chair began rocking back and forth.

"It was just like the chair rocked when Mama rocked my baby brother," Jennie's mother told her later. "It felt like Mama had stopped on her way to Heaven to tell me good-bye."

The years passed, and Jennie's mother grew elderly. Even though she was still alive, it was Jennie's turn to inherit the family rocking chair, which she kept in her bedroom.

"I was working on a deadline for a book and couldn't get the story to go together, and I had been up until about 1:30 in the morning," Jennie said. "When I went to bed, everyone else was already asleep. I turned out the light in my office, and then I made my way to my room, but I didn't turn on any lights. I just threw my clothes in the rocking chair. As I did, I realized that there was already a lot of stuff sitting there. I found out later that my husband had already left a pile of books and papers on it before he went to bed.

"I had been asleep for about half an hour when I heard my mother's voice say, 'How do you expect me to sit on that chair when there's so much clutter on it?'

"My eyes popped open, and I jumped out of bed and cleared off the chair in a hurry.

"Just then the phone rang, and it was my sister calling to tell me that Mom had died."

Jennie found that at the funeral, as well as afterward, relatives would look for opportunities to ask her about the chair. "My sister and several of my cousins all contacted me very privately and asked if I had seen the chair rock."

Yet family curiosity over the chair doesn't necessarily translate to interest in ownership. Two of Jennie's daughters have specifically requested that they not inherit the chair either before or after their mother dies. "But my third daughter wants it," Jennie said. "And if she changes her mind, my youngest daughter said she would like to have it."

Guardian Angel

They're always there for you.

Darcy pulled back the covers, punched the ends of her pillow in toward the middle, and climbed into bed. She glanced at the book that waited for her on the bedside stand, but decided she was too tired to read.

Still, she couldn't go to sleep because she could hear her eighteen-year-old sister, Jo, splashing around at the bathroom sink.

Darcy felt a twinge of annoyance. Ever since she'd moved to Lethbridge, Canada, with her mother and sisters, twenty-two year old Darcy had shared a room with Jo, their parallel twin beds set like double exclamation marks against one wall with their dressers set as the dots against the opposite wall. It was a tolerable arrangement, for the most part, except that she was always ready for bed before her sister, even if she offered to let Jo use the bathroom first.

Darcy settled back into her pillow and closed her eyes, wondering if she might be able to fall asleep before Jo got done. The answer was no. When Jo clicked open the bathroom door, a slice of light cut their room in two. Darcy's eyes flew open just before Jo snapped the light off, plunging the room into murky darkness illuminated only by the faint glow of the streetlight trying to peek through the closed shutters.

Jo shuffled over to her bedside. The springs creaked as Jo knelt down, elbows propped on her mattress, to say her nightly prayer.

Darcy sighed and turned away, pulling the covers up over her shoulder and facing their bedroom door. Darcy didn't even bother to close her eyes. She poised on the edge of wakefulness, waiting for her sister to settle in so she could relax into sleep.

The streetlight began glowing brighter, as though someone was opening the shutters. What was Jo up to now?

Darcy threw an annoyed looked over her shoulder at Jo, a brusque question at the ready. When she saw Jo's blonde head still bowed over her folded hands, Darcy bit her lips and remained silent. A quick glance at the window proved that the shutters were still closed.

Puzzled, Darcy turned back toward the door. The corner up against the ceiling was noticeably lighter than it had been before, almost like Jo was playing around with a flashlight that had nearly spent its battery.

But Jo was still saying her prayers.

Darcy stared at the spot that continued to lighten until, to her astonishment, the shape of a woman materialized in the light. Her outline from the waist up grew more distinct as Darcy watched in wide-eyed fascination. The woman appeared to be in her thirties. Her hands were folded gently in front of her waist. "She had long, blondish hair the same color as Jo's, and she was watching Jo with an expression of absolute love on her face," Darcy said.

The woman stayed where she was, the top of her head nearly touching the ceiling, until Jo pushed herself up off of her knees and climbed into bed. Darcy watched as the woman in the corner bowed her head, closed her eyes, and de-materialized. The room was now as dark as before.

"Jo!" Darcy called out in excitement, turning toward her sister.

"What?"

"I just saw your guardian angel."

Jo shot up in bed. "Where?"

Darcy pointed. "She was there. While you were saying your prayers, she was there watching you."

Jo glanced up at the empty corner for a quiet moment before she whispered, "Darcy?"

"Yes?"

"I've been praying for two weeks to know if I had a guardian angel. Just now, I was asking again."

"Well, you do," Darcy said, "Because I saw her."

Child Care

Who visits the handicapped boy when he's all alone?

In 1990, Dyana's sister, Sharyn, agreed to help Dyana pack up her belongings so she could move out of a house on the outskirts of a small rural town. "There were a lot of flies out there, and the smell of poultry farms was awful," Dyana said. "I was glad to be going." Dyana assigned Sharyn the task of boxing up the kitchen items while Dyana got busy folding linens into boxes as quickly as she could.

Suddenly, a little boy ran past Dyana, into the back room and into the closet.

Since she had two young daughters who often played with friends, Dyana kept on working for a few moments, her mind preoccupied with all the things she still had to do. But then she stopped in mid-fold. The running child had been absolutely silent. His pounding feet hadn't made a sound. The strangeness of the event hit Dyana all at once, and the hair on the back of her neck rose.

Wait a minute! Who was that? Dropping the towel she'd been folding, Dyana walked toward the closet. There was no sound or movement from within. Goosebumps raced up her arms as she reached toward the closet door. With a growing certainty that she had seen something extraordinary, Dyana pulled the door wide open. The closet was empty.

Dyana felt her whole body tingle, as though her spirit

stretched beyond the confines of her body, triggering a strange emotion that welled up inside, wringing Dyana's heart until she suddenly burst into tears.

"My sister came in and asked what was wrong," Dyana said. "I told her, 'Just feel this.'"

"What?"

Dyana paused, spread both hands out with the backs up, and pulsed her palms downward to emphasize each word. "Just feel this." Sharyn stopped for a minute, her eyes searching her sister's face. Then she burst into tears too.

Dyana believes that the little boy on silent feet had a mighty spirit, so strong it touched the souls of the two women and made them cry.

Dyana's found plenty of reasons to cry over the years. She's had to deal with premature babies, infant meningitis, and infant heart problems. When she was at her weariest, she'd often pray, asking, "What are You preparing me for?"

She finally found out after the fourteen-week-premature birth of her youngest child, Nat. He wasn't supposed to live, but he did. Once she learned to feed him through a feeding tube, Dyana was able to bring her fragile son home from the hospital.

Late one night, when they were the only two awake in the house, Dyana was feeding Nat, when she said she "got a sudden warm feeling. I thought, *Oh my gosh, this is what I've been preparing for all my life.*"

It turned out that Nat's myriad medical problems included a serious mental handicap. "To put it simply, he has cerebral palsy," Dyana said. "The doctors said the left half of his brain is like it was cremated. He's legally blind. He babbles." Although the doctors predicted that he never would walk, at nine years old, Nat can totter around the house. It's a much different gait than the one of the mysterious boy who used to run through the house, but perhaps the silent running boy was Nat, giving his mother a glimpse of what he was truly like.

"Nat has brought a very strong spirit into our home," Dyana said. "I think it's like a force field he has that keeps bad things out. Satan can't touch him. The only way Heavenly Father could send him to earth was to make him a protected soul. Nat has spiritual things happen to him all the time."

Although he has very few words, most of which are mostly unintelligible, Dyana says, "He talks in the middle of the night. He'll be sitting up, wide awake, talking as if having a conversation with someone, but with words I don't understand." When Dyana goes to check on her son, she never sees anyone he could be talking to.

There are occasions when Nat is playing alone and his sister, Tara, hears him laugh for no apparent reason. "He's on his back, and it's like someone's tickling him or something," Tara said.

On one particularly memorable occasion, Tara and Nat were the only ones home. Tara was in the kitchen doing dishes when she heard a boy's voice from the other room as plain as day, speaking actual words, although too far away for her to make out what was being said. She wondered who else was there, since she and Nat were the only ones home as far as she knew. With some trepidation, she went to investigate.

Nat was alone. Tara checked the rest of the house, just to be sure. Everything was as it should be. As far as Tara could tell, they were the only two people in the house.

Puzzled, Tara went back to the room where Nat waited. He looked up at her and grinned but didn't say a word.

A Wall of Mist

What stopped the toddler from tumbling into the frigid water?

Victoria stared in amazement at the pint-sized Victorian style coat in the store display. It was the very image of a coat her father had worn as a boy, and was just the right size of her one-year-old son, Courtland. Victoria bought the coat. It fit Courtland perfectly, and she never tired of seeing him wear it.

By the time spring of 2002 rolled around, Victoria was disappointed to see that Courtland had grown so much he'd never be able to wear the coat for next winter. When she told her friend, Gloria Healy, that she would miss seeing Courtland in the coat, Gloria suggested that they take some pictures of him with it on. Gloria was already very fond of the little boy. "I felt a special connection with Courtland even before he was born," Gloria said.

While she was pregnant, someone told Victoria that Courtland was a girl, but Gloria thought differently. She warned Victoria not to be surprised if the baby turned out to be a boy. Gloria was right.

"Courtland calls me Grandma Gloria. He's really bright, way beyond normal measures," Gloria said.

Victoria was pleased at the idea of taking pictures. Since Courtland resembled her father, she decided that she'd give her father a photograph of Courtland wearing the coat.

Snow in the valley was in short supply that April, so the

two women drove up into the mountains in search of snow, which is the only proper setting for a picture with a coat. The only snow they found was an undisturbed patch nestled under a tree, next to a river full of icy spring run-off water. There was a rock set right in the center of the snow, just the right size for a makeshift chair.

The women pulled over to the side of the road and got out of the car. Victoria had recently broken her ankle, but it had healed to the point that she was able to walk on it. She carried her eighteen-month-old son over to the rock and set him on top. Then she stepped back so Gloria could get a clear view of Courtland through her camera viewfinder.

Things went well for several frames. Courtland smiled adorably, while in the sunlight beyond the shade, the water sparkled and laughed its way in between the frozen banks. Yet it doesn't take long for an eighteen-month-old to use up his attention span, so when Courtland decided he'd had enough, he slid off the rock and ran toward the enticing sound of the river.

Gloria screamed and hurried toward the boy. Victoria was closer and raced for her son, but the weight of her frantic body pounding down on her barely healed ankle was too much.

"I heard a crack," Gloria said. "I thought she'd stepped on a stick."

Victoria's ankle was broken again, but she refused to stop. She hobbled toward her son, who had not slowed down but looked as though he intended to jump headlong into the freezing water.

As a sick, cold feeling grabbed her heart, Victoria realized that she could not possibly reach her son in time to stop him from tumbling into a river that rumbled like a freight train between the snowy banks. She was so close, though, she couldn't give up. She kept going, fueled by a mother's undying determination to save her son.

Just as Courtland reached a point of no return, where his own momentum could only carry him over the side of the slippery bank, a mist rose up from the surface of the clear water and spread out before him. Courtland stopped so abruptly, it was as if a hand pushed against his chest. He teetered on the edge of the river for a moment, so close that he might have gotten the toes of his shoes wet.

"It was like he hit a roadblock, and he backed up," Victoria said. "If he'd fallen in, he would have been gone. Whatever it was just rose out of the water. It was like he hit a brick wall."

There was no fog on the river. Everything had been perfectly clear until Courtland's race to the water's edge.

The grateful mother reached her son and scooped him up into her arms. Gloria finally reached her side, tears running down her cheeks. She helped Victoria to the car where the two of them offered up a prayer of heartfelt thanks before they drove home.

Gloria took her hard-earned roll of film to the store for developing. When she went back to get the pictures, no one could find them anywhere, although several people looked.

It was with keen disappointment that Gloria left the store, but she had to tell herself that it was better to lose a few pictures than to lose the life of a child.

Two years later, Gloria went to the same film department to pick up some other prints. Since the camera bar was closed, the store manager agreed to go behind the counter to look for her order. Being unfamiliar with the department, he rummaged around for a bit in a box behind the counter before he came up with an envelope with Gloria's name on it. But inside, she didn't see the pictures she was expecting.

"He found the old pictures I'd taken of Courtland," Gloria said. Seeing them again brought back all the memories of the day by the snow bank. Gloria knew what she had to do. "I had one framed for Christmas for Victoria."

Neither of the women has any idea what the mist was. Neither one knows why it stopped the little boy on the very brink of disaster, but they don't lose any sleep over it, because they aren't about to question a miracle.

Grandma's Unfinished Business

Grandma hadn't done everything she wanted to do before she died.

Kimberley Huffaker visited Grandma Fern every night at nine. She only stayed about an hour, but it was an hour well spent. Kimberley enjoyed her grandma's company, and Grandma returned the feeling, creating a close relationship between them.

Although not entirely unexpected, Grandma's death left Kimberley unsettled. She would go through her daily routine, yet each night just before nine o'clock, she'd catch herself heading for the door. Only then would she remember that Grandma wasn't there to visit anymore. Would she ever get used to it?

A week after Grandma died, Kimberley decided that she really had to go to Grandma's house to find a set of keys for her aunt and uncle. "I was planning to go over early to do it," Kimberley said. "But the day wore on, and for whatever reason, I went over there at nine o'clock PM like I usually did."

Kimberley parked her car in front of Grandma's, and, as usual, went through the garage toward the door that led into the house, but she didn't go through it. "Instead of going into the house, I started picking things up in the garage," Kimberley said. "I picked a small rug up from the floor, rolled it up, and put it on a shelf. Then I heard Grandma say, 'Kimberley, make sure to put that oil additive in the trunk of the car' like she had said so many times when she was alive. I said out loud, 'Okay, Grandma, I hear you,' and did what I was told."

Kimberley wasn't startled by her grandmother's voice. It seems that a sixth sense runs in the family. "My mother's father's sister, Aunt Myrt, had a second sight," Kimberley said. "She would bake a cake because she felt like family was coming, and, sure enough, someone would come from Montana or wherever."

Aunt Myrt wasn't the only one to experience unusual insight. "There are funny things on Mom's side of the family," Kimberley said. "Aunt Myrt's first husband, Pat, was killed on the job fairly early in his life. Grandpa Charlie was getting up there in age, but he wasn't sick or mentally challenged by his years. One day, Grandpa was sitting there when he looked up and said, 'Well, hell, Pat, what's going on? You're dead. What're you doing here?'"

Later, Grandpa explained that Pat had been standing there as plain as day. Grandpa meant to strike up a conversation with him, but then he realized he couldn't because Pat was dead.

Now Kimberley was hearing instruction from Grandma, who wasn't really there. Kimberley wasn't surprised, though. Says Kimberly, "I speak to my relatives who've passed. I'll say, 'Grandpa, I've got to fix this machine. You've got to help me.' Then I'll walk away and when I come back, I'll see what I need to do, and it works. Whether it's them helping me or a fresh perspective, I don't know."

With the additive safely in the trunk of Grandma's car, Kimberley felt like she could go inside to look for the keys. Knowing Grandma, the most logical place to find them would be the kitchen, but instead of stopping at the kitchen drawers, Kimberley went to Grandma's bedroom. She was drawn to Grandma's chest of drawers. "I'd not been in Grandma's dresser for ten years," Kimberley said.

She pulled out a drawer, reached into the back of it, and pulled out three dishtowels. When she examined them, she saw that they were hand-embroidered with pictures of cats. "My sister was always known as Katrina the cat," Kimberley said. "She had three children, and there were three cat towels." The meaning was clear to Kimberley. Grandma wanted Katrina to have the towels for her children.

"I didn't have any idea that those were in that drawer," Kimberley said. "But as soon as I pulled them out, I knew what I was supposed to do with them."

Then Kimberley went to get the keys, happy that she'd been able to help Grandma finish up a couple of things she hadn't had time to get to before she died.

The Night Mom Said Good-bye

Loved ones don't stop caring about us after they die.

"My mother died in the spring of 1981, just four months after I was married," said Susan Miller. "I rode down to southern California with some relatives a couple of days before the funeral so that I could help my dad and sisters go through Mom's things."

Since the relatives were given the bedrooms for the night, Susan and her sister Lauren ended up in sleeping bags rolled out on the living room floor. As sisters often do, they stayed up late into the night to talk.

"Lauren and I were talking about memories that we had, both good and bad. At one point, I looked over toward the stairs. At first I thought that a streetlight was shining in through the window because there was an illuminated spot right there."

But Susan soon changed her mind. "I looked closer and saw that the white shadow had my mother's features. When I first realized it was a person, I thought it was my other sister, Jennette, sitting there in her white bathrobe and listening in."

Susan pointed out the apparition to Lauren, and the two of them discussed the matter in cautious whispers. They soon decided that it couldn't be Jennette sitting there. They wondered if it could actually be their mother's spirit.

"It made my palms sweat. I have never seen a ghost before."

The sisters talked on, casting uneasy glances at the ghost on the stairs.

Finally, Susan confessed to Lauren that she had to go to the bathroom. "But the only way to get to the bathroom was to walk past the staircase," Susan said.

Afraid that a close up view of the ghost might prove to have a horror movie appearance, Susan made Lauren get up and go with her. Locking arms, the sisters drew abreast of the ghost.

"Mom was wearing the dress that Lauren had just finished that day for her to be buried in," Susan said. "It made Lauren feel really good, because Mom had accepted it." Their mother had bought the fabric before she died, but had become too weak to actually sew anything.

By the time the sisters returned from the bathroom, the staircase was empty.

"That's okay," Lauren said. "She really ought to be hanging around Dad to comfort him anyway."

Susan saw her mother once more, a few years later. "I was sad about not having any children," Susan said. "I was in the bathroom getting ready for work, and out of the corner of my eye I saw someone standing behind me, and it looked like my mother. When I turned around to look at her straight on, I couldn't see anyone." For a moment, Susan was confused, wondering if she'd really seen her mother in the mirror. "Then this scripture popped into my head, about 'to everything there is a season and a time to every purpose under heaven.' Then I knew it was Mom, who had come to give me a message of comfort."

Dad, You're Dead

Unyielding in life, stubborn in death, Dad was pretty upset that no one was listening to him anymore.

"Dad didn't believe in God," Jason Bradley said. "But he did believe that he would live forever."

Carl Bradley was what some people might call a hard man. He was so certain that his way was the right way that he wouldn't tolerate anyone else expressing a different opinion. He was "the man in charge" for so long that when he suffered a heart attack, it took him completely by surprise.

He wasn't the least bit humbled when he woke up in a recovery room. The experience didn't improve his disposition any, either. He continued to be a curmudgeon. "Dad was a very strong willed and hard-headed person whose mind couldn't be changed once he had it set on something," Jason said.

Several months later, a second heart attack interrupted Carl's life. "His heart stopped for a few minutes," Jason said. "He claimed he never saw anything of any life after this one. When it was all over and he was on his way to recovering again, he seemed even more convinced that he could not die."

He was wrong.

Carl finally succumbed to heart failure in August 2001. At least, that's what Jason was told.

"Dad died in Asia," Jason said. "It's my understanding that

the Asians really didn't bother to do an autopsy. They just declared that he died of heart failure. That's quite possible, but some people in my family suspect that his Asian wife may have poisoned him. It really wouldn't surprise me."

At his father's funeral, instead of mourning, Jason felt a certain measure of relief. The years of living under his father's stern dictatorship were done. Overall, Carl had been an unwelcome force in Jason's life. His sweeping sense of disapproval had brushed cold fingers of discontent over Jason many times, ever since Jason was a boy, and even after Jason grew up and took his young family home for a visit. Even thinking about his father had made Jason tense.

Now he was free.

Or so he thought.

Two months after the funeral, Jason saw his father again, in a most disturbing dream, with a different feel than a conventional one.

Jason had dreamed like this before, mostly when he was a teenager. "I knew stuff, like the time when my girlfriend was going to break up with me," Jason said. "I had this dream, and the very next day, I waited all day long for her to come and talk to me. Sure enough, when she walked up to me at the end of the day, I knew what she was going to say. It was just like my dream. I hated it. It would have been better not to know beforehand."

In spite of the remembered agony of knowing that his heart was headed for a fracture, Jason has discovered that he feels better when he gets occasional premonitions. If a lot of time goes by without any, Jason feels empty and incomplete. "Having these dreams and interactions doesn't seem odd or strange to me," Jason said. "I've had several dreams that have come true. I can tell a difference between regular dreams and visions or premonitions that I get while I'm asleep."

Carl never thought much of his son's unique dreaming ability while he was alive, but he seemed to finally appreciate it in death.

"I met Dad in one of my vision-dreams a couple of months after his funeral," Jason said.

Carl stood in front of his son, as imposing a figure now as he'd been in life. "Why won't anyone talk to me?" Carl demanded.

Jason was taken aback. His father's stance, the familiar crease of disapproval slashed across his forehead, even his voice, rich with irritation, made Jason wince. Stunned, he didn't answer right away.

"Well?" Carl yelled. "Tell me why everyone's ignoring me!"

"Dad," Jason said. "You're dead."

The silence that followed was awful. Carl glared holes through his son, lowering his brow until his eyes nearly disappeared. Then he opened his mouth to speak, and his words came out in a low growl. "I am not dead."

Jason spread his hands. "I went to your funeral last November."

Carl folded his arms across his ribs and tipped his chin up. "Then why am I standing here talking to you?"

"It's just a dream," Jason said, unsure of the fact until he heard his own words.

Jason felt a subtle shift as Carl faded away and Jason came awake in his bed. The oppressive sense of not measuring up to Dad's expectations pressed heavy on his heart.

As he went through the day, he reflected on his father's dilemma. "It was interesting to imagine him trying to interact with others and getting no response," Jason said. "It must have been frustrating and depressing."

Over a period of several months, Jason met his father a few more times.

"I kept trying to explain to him that he was dead. His difficulty in believing he'd died may be due in part to the fact that if he ever did see an error in his judgment, it was rare for him to admit it."

One night, Carl grew angrier than he'd ever been before.

"Shut up!" he roared at Jason. "Don't you dare tell me I'm dead! Don't say that again, do you hear me?"

"He was extremely upset with me, yet this time, I felt he'd finally accepted the truth," Jason said.

Carl didn't come back to see Jason for quite a while after that angry encounter. But he did come back.

"This last time, I met him at his place of business, the one he'd had when he was alive," Jason said. Jason was vaguely aware of two figures in white hovering in the background. Even though he didn't focus his attention on them, he got the sense that they were his father's spirit guides.

Carl's demeanor was different on this visit. He asked his son questions about marriage, of all things, and the importance of it. "He has difficulty with this concept, which is not surprising, since he certainly was not good at being faithful while he was alive," Jason said.

Carl seemed much more calm and approachable now that he'd accepted his death.

"I also had dreams of my father after his funeral that were nothing more than commonplace dreams," Jason said. "But those in which he approached me, requesting help and venting his frustration over not being able to communicate with others, felt different. They felt just like my premonitions that always came true."

It took more than a lifetime for Carl to finally listen to his son. Now that Jason has been able to convince his father that he's dead, he's hopeful that his father will continue to progress, and perhaps even visit him again sometime.

What Dad Doesn't See

Some unseen beings keep using the stairs and easy chairs.

It's ironic that after David's family moved into his ancestral home on April 1, 1991, it was David's wife and daughters who experienced the supernatural events.

"I was raised in this house," David said. "And the only scary thing that happened to me was when me and my cousin were boys and we were upstairs in bed. The house was creaking, so we got scared and came downstairs. Then my dad made us sleep in different parts of the house."

Apparently, Dad didn't like being disturbed in the night, but now that David's parents are dead, can some strange events be blamed on his restless mother?

More than one of David's girls have heard footsteps going up and down the stairs and pacing the floors at night. "That's Grandma Eulula," David's twenty-three-year-old daughter, Jacquie, explained.

"I'm not so sure it's my mother-in-law," said David's wife, Diane. "But sometimes I get a whiff of her perfume. One night when I heard the creak of footsteps going across the floor, I got up to see who it was. I couldn't see anything, but I could hear someone walking in the living room. My mother-in-law was an insomniac. She used to pace the floor, then sit in the rocking chair and rock."

If it is Grandma Eulula, it appears that she's not the only ghost using the staircase.

"I've heard children running up and down the stairs when I've been home alone," Jacquie said. "They're laughing, talking, and giggling."

Nineteen-year-old Jamie has seen evidence of Grandpa Joe, too. "When we had Grandpa's chair in here, it would rock," she said.

Diane disagrees. "The rocking chair was Grandma. The recliner is Grandpa," she said.

One night, Jacquie saw someone standing in her bedroom doorway. "It was a great big guy, just a black figure, like a shadow," she said. At first, she felt a shock of fear. "Your physical body is not prepared or made to see those things, so your body goes through a shock when it sees stuff like that," she said.

Still, once she got over the initial surprise, Jacquie says, "I never felt afraid of him." She said that she's seen him in a couple of other places that she's lived but hasn't seen him for about a year now.

Diane seems to have seen the same apparition. "There's a big man always dressed in white in our home. I don't get good glimpses of him. I look up, and there he is, and then he's gone. He's tall, well-built, and muscular. He gives me the impression of David's father. This man watches over us."

Another daughter, Tiffany, has also seen this ghost. "There's a big guy upstairs," she said. "He's tall. I haven't seen his face, because he's shadowy. He doesn't stand there like, 'Grrr.'" Tiffany made a menacing posture, with her knees bent, arms at her sides, and hands curled into fists. Then she straightened up. "He stands like a protective person. He's not scary."

No one in the family is sure why Dad doesn't see the ghosts. "I can't help but wonder if some things happen that are connected to people, because nothing ever happens to Dad," Jacquie said.

"Yeah, the ghosts like Dad, so they never bother him," Tiffany added.

"David is not a believer," Diane said. "I think some people are more sensitive."

"There are days when we've walked inside after being gone, and doors or windows are open that we know were shut and locked," Jacquie said. "We've walked into this house and just known someone's there. There's a gift of sight, a gift of hearing, and a gift of sense. Dad just doesn't get it."

I Was the Ghost

How could the teenager, resting in his bed at home, see his father at work?

Roland Puili was seventeen years old when his father worked as a bartender. Part of his dad's responsibility was to count the money at the end of every evening, a job that often kept him from home until two o'clock AM.

One night, Roland was sleeping soundly when his mother came into his room. "Roland! Wake up! Your father's not home yet and I'm worried about him," she said. "Please go and see if he's all right."

Roland tried to open his eyes, but the hall light was so bright he could only manage to squint up at his mother. "What time is it?"

"Nearly four o'clock AM." Mom wrung her hands in front of her faded nightgown. "He's never been this late before."

"Okay, Mom," the groggy teenager said. "I'll go check it out."

"I'll get the car keys while you get dressed." Roland's mother hurried out of the room.

Roland relaxed back into his pillow and closed his eyes again. He wasn't going back to sleep, he told himself, he just wanted to wake up more slowly.

The next thing Roland knew, he was standing outside the bar where his father worked. Although he hadn't expected to be there so soon, he wasn't alarmed. There was something he needed to do there.

He looked up to see his father's office window. It was too high for him to look into from where he stood at street level, so with his teenage agility, Roland hoisted himself up onto a ledge beneath the window.

As soon as Roland got his balance, he moved his face closer to the window glass. There was a lamp on his father's desk. A yellow pool of light illuminated his father's head, which lay motionless on the desktop. A pen lay an inch or two away from his still fingers. A sheaf of papers was his pillow. The cash box was open, green bills edging into the light like shy forest creatures.

Roland's attention focused on his father. He viewed the still man without fear. Somehow he knew that his father was not dead, nor even injured, but merely sleeping.

Suddenly, Roland was back in his room. He sat up in bed, startled by what he'd just seen. It was so real, he knew it wasn't a dream. Somehow, his spirit had left his body when he'd let himself rest for a few moments, and had gone to check on his father.

Roland swung his legs out from under his covers and pulled on a pair of pants. Footsteps in the hall signaled his mother's return.

"Here you go," his mother said, pushing a set of car keys toward him.

"Mom, Dad's all right," Roland said, taking the keys in his hand.

Mom narrowed her eyes. "How do you know?"

"I just do. He fell asleep at his desk. He's okay."

"Oh, I hope you're right," Mom said, putting one hand up to her face.

"We'll be back soon," Roland said.

When Roland arrived at the bar, he found everything exactly as he had seen it just a few minutes earlier. He climbed up on the ledge and looked in. His dad was surrounded by the tools of his trade while he slept in a pool of yellow light, just as Roland had seen him before. But this time, Roland rapped on the window. In short order, both father and son were safely home.

And Roland has never haunted anyone since.

Waiting Upstairs

Sometimes the worst thing is not knowing.

"I always felt like somebody was up there," Gigi said of the second floor in the house she lives in now. "Even before I married John, I could feel it."

The family home, built in the 1800s, had been lived in and looked after by John and his brother, Drew, since Grandma Cora had gone to live in a nursing home. Both of the young men were bachelors, but John soon began dating Gigi and bringing her home. Gigi liked being with John, but she didn't like something that she sensed in his house.

"Any time I went up to the second floor, it felt like somebody was there," Gigi said. "I was always scared to go upstairs."

Gigi didn't feel any malice from the unseen presence, but it made her uneasy not knowing who was up there, or why. "I've always been able to sense things," Gigi said. "I can tell when people are telling the truth. I can tell what they really think of me. I can tell when there are spirits around, but most of the time I don't want to tune in to them because I get scared. I don't know if I'll see something bad or something good, so I mostly just want them to leave me alone."

Eventually, John and Gigi were married. Grandma Cora didn't make it to the wedding because of her poor health.

Gigi still wanted to meet her, so John promised he would take her to visit someday.

When Gigi moved in, Drew moved out, and Gigi set about making the place her own. She pulled up carpet, painted walls, moved a doorway, and tiled a section of wall to prepare for a woodstove.

In due time, John and Gigi had a son named Jason. Yet Gigi's apprehension about the second floor had not eased over the passing months.

"I never felt in danger or anything, I just felt like somebody was watching," Gigi said. "You'd get the creepies where the hair stands up on the back of your neck, and you'd get cold. Every time I went up there I'd feel that."

One chilly December day, Gigi had to go upstairs to get something. Again she felt someone watching her. In frustration she yelled, "What do you want?" before running back downstairs to safety.

That night, Gigi had a dream. An older woman with a pleasant face approached her, followed closely by a middle-aged man. "Hello, my dear," the woman said. "I'm John's great-grandmother, Eloise, and this is his Grandpa Dean." The man nodded and grinned.

Gigi felt a catch in her heart. Dean was the name of Cora's husband, who'd died several years earlier.

The woman clasped her hands at her waist and leaned toward Gigi. "We've been watching you," she said, with a slight smile that could have been an apology. "We just wanted to make sure that you would take care of this home."

"You're a special girl," Dean said, nodding his head. Gigi wondered what he meant. Had they been there the day she'd accused John of hiding cigarettes in his coat pocket after he swore he'd quit smoking? She had no reason to suspect the cigarettes were there. She just knew.

John had stared at her with something close to awe in his eyes. "Are you psychic?"

Gigi didn't bother to answer him. She just went out to

the truck where his coat was, fished the cigarettes out of the pocket, and destroyed them.

Eloise spoke again. "Now we know that you'll take good care of John and Jason," she said, her smile brightening in approval. "We just wanted you to know that we're leaving now to sit by Cora's bedside, because it's her time to go."

Dean gave Gigi and little wave just before he and Eloise faded away.

"This was in late December," Gigi remembered. "About two weeks later, in January, we were headed to my brother's wedding in Washington. I told John that I wanted to stop and see Grandma Cora on the way."

Even though John said there wasn't enough time, Gigi persisted, reminding John that she'd prayed to get to meet his grandma. John finally relented.

A small circle of family members, including John and Gigi, stood around Grandma's bed. Gigi felt an instant connection to the frail old woman. "She'd look around the circle with a confused look in her eyes, but when her eyes lit on me, she smiled," Gigi said. Cora also gave Gigi a little nod, as though she recognized her.

It turned out to be Gigi's last chance to meet Grandma Cora. "After we got to Washington, we got a phone call saying that she'd passed away."

As soon as she heard the news, a fleeting impression flashed through Gigi's mind of a grinning Dean folding a laughing Cora into his arms.

Don't Be Frightened

When great-great-Grandpa came, one sister hid in fear while the other felt at peace.

Candace was seventeen years old when her mother and father found out she was dying. "The doctors told my parents that if I got stressed out, I could die sooner," Candace said, "so they didn't tell me the diagnosis."

The heart tests showed that Candace was missing two branches of her pulmonary artery. The left side of her heart had atrophied, and she needed surgery.

Because of her heart condition, Candace always slept deeply through the night. But one night in 1981, she woke out of a sound sleep to see a man standing at the foot of her bed. He appeared to be in his late fifties and wore a top hat and clothes similar to those of the 1860s. "I wasn't scared," Candace said. "Neither one of us said anything, and after a moment, I just went back to sleep."

Eventually, Candace had successful heart surgery. But her nighttime visitor kept coming, even after she moved away to go to college.

"Periodically over the next ten years, I'd wake up to see the same man standing by my bed," Candace said. She never spoke to him. She'd wake up long enough to see him watching over her, then she'd go back to sleep.

One day, when Candace was twenty-seven and her little sister Heather was twenty, they were driving home to Dolores, Colorado, with their cousin David for the Thanksgiving holiday. The cousins discussed many things during the long drive. At one point, Heather brought up a childhood memory of a night when she woke up and saw a strange man standing by her bed. She was so scared that she dove under the covers and didn't come out until morning.

The memory struck a chord in Candace and she asked, "What did he look like?"

Heather proceeded to describe her visitor, from the top hat on down. He sounded so familiar that Candace probed for more information. The sisters finally determined that the night Heather saw the man was the same night that Candace first saw him at the foot of her bed. The sisters' bedrooms were not only adjoining, but Heather had to go through Candace's room to reach the main part of the house.

Now they were more excited than ever to get home. As soon as the car pulled up in front of the house, the sisters hopped out and ran inside. They told their mother what had happened. Intrigued, their mother started digging through her store of family pictures. She found an old photo and turned it toward the girls.

"That looks like him," Candace said doubtfully.

"But it's not quite right," Heather added.

"This is a picture of your great-great-grandfather," Mom told them.

After a brief discussion, the women quickly figured out that the spirit must have been the pictured man's father, George Lynch, born in Ireland in 1823.

"Did you ask him what he wanted?" Mom asked.

Heather shook her head. "No, I never saw him after that first time. I never wanted to."

"I've seen him lots of times," Candace said.

They determined that Grandpa George must be the girls' guardian angel, but since his visit had scared Heather so much, he'd never appeared to her again. Candace only felt peace and calm when she saw him, so he'd apparently been more willing to let her know when he was checking in on her.

Candace was excited. "I'll ask him what he wants next time," she said.

With this resolve firmly in her mind, Candace has never seen him since.

List of Questions

A father gets miraculous help from the other side.

Bryce Olsen was working as a fireman in 1972 when he found himself in the midst of a messy divorce from his first wife. "My first wife was playing around a lot," Olsen said.

Because of the moral circumstances, he felt that he should be the one to get custody of their children. "The only thing I could do was go to court to take the kids away from her," he said. But the odds of the father getting custody were practically non-existent in the early 1970s.

"The lawyer said, 'You don't stand a chance of getting these kids,'" Olsen remembers. "It was pretty rough back then, because they always gave the kids to the woman."

It didn't sound like much of a chance.

One day, Olsen had an experience that firmed his resolve to fight for his children. "I was getting ready to build a house," Olsen said. "I jacked this little building up that I had to move, and then I crawled around underneath and got it up around sixteen inches off the ground. Then it tipped off the blocks."

Olsen grabbed hold of a joist, figuring that if he could get in between a couple of joists, then he had a chance to survive. "I just knew I was going to die," he said. But before he could put his swiftly concocted plan into action, the building stopped tipping. "It stopped on the blocks that were eight inches off the ground, and that kept it from crushing me. I dug myself out. That experience let me know that I could have been taken, but that I stayed here because I had something to do."

Olsen decided to take action, and his child custody case was finally brought to court in 1975.

The day before the court hearing was scheduled, Olsen was at work in the firehouse. He knew full well that he was facing the prospect of an $8,000 lawyer bill if he failed to win the case and had to pay his ex-wife's court costs. It was a daunting thought.

Tense and worried about the outcome, Olsen decided to turn to prayer. But he wanted a private place.

"I went into the men's room and I prayed about it," Olsen said. "All of a sudden the room lit up bright, and a voice spoke to me and said, 'Discouragement is a tool of the devil.' I thought, *this is weird*."

Olsen left the men's room and walked around the fire station, thinking about what had just happened. He began to think that maybe he'd imagined it, so he went back into the bathroom and prayed again.

The same thing happened.

"I thought it was so loud that the whole department could hear it, but only I could," he said.

This time Olsen got more information. "I was impressed that I had to ask questions of my youngest daughter. I wrote them down as they came to me. There were twenty-three questions, and then it stopped. That was it."

The next day, dressed in a suit and sitting stiffly in a hard backed chair, Olsen faced his lawyer.

"Are you sure you want to do this?" his lawyer asked.

Olsen looked him in the eye. "There's no question."

Olsen was not permitted to go into the judge's chambers while his children were interviewed, so he handed the list of questions that he'd written down the previous day to his lawyer.

"What's this?" his lawyer asked, glancing at the paper.

"I want you to ask these questions of my youngest daughter," Olsen explained.

"I don't need those. I've got my own questions," the lawyer said, but he slipped Olsen's paper into his pocket anyway.

Olsen's children disappeared into the judge's chambers, and the door shut behind them. It felt like the door had closed on Olsen's heart.

He sat and waited, clasping and unclasping his hands. It seemed an eternity before the door finally opened again. Olsen anxiously searched each face, looking for some clue as to what the verdict might be.

"When the judge, the lawyers, and the kids came back out, the judge asked one more question and slammed the gavel down to award me all the children," Olsen said.

Later, Olsen asked his lawyer what had happened.

"We went into the judge's chamber, and I was tongue-tied," the lawyer said. "I couldn't think of what to say. I couldn't find my notes. The only thing I found was your paper with the questions, so I used those."

"The questions were along moral lines," Olsen said. "I know it was somebody from the other side who was helping us, and I'll be interested to find out who it was someday."

Spirits All around Us

When you tune in, you get all kinds of help.

When Bryce Olsen drove through Montana on his way to his mother's funeral in 1995, he caught himself drifting toward the shoulder of the road. "I couldn't stay awake," he said, "so I pulled over and went to sleep for two hours. I woke up at about three AM and tried to start my diesel pickup truck, but it wouldn't turn over. So I offered up a prayer. I said, 'Mom, if you can hear me, send me some help.'"

After about six minutes of watching cars go by, a big, brand new semi-truck pulled over. The driver had noticed Olsen's raised hood and asked if he needed help.

"He jump-started my truck and got me going," Olsen said. "I tried to pay him, but he wouldn't take it."

Olsen got back on the road with the semi's headlights plainly visible in his rearview mirror. "I slowed down so I could give him a high sign," Olsen said. "A car went by me, and a couple of other trucks went past, but I don't know where he went. He just disappeared."

When Olsen got to Utah, he found out that both batteries in his truck were shot. Neither one of them would work.

Olsen wouldn't be surprised if the truck driver who helped him was really an angel.

"I've had things like that happen quite a few times," Olsen said. "My brother-in-law taught me how to put in central vacuum systems, but he died when he was only forty. The interesting thing is, now I can do difficult jobs that no one else can do. People say, 'I don't know how you did that,' and I say, 'I don't know either.' The difference is that I ask for help. My brother-in-law will come to me and put it right in my mind how to do things that I can't figure out. Other people may not understand this, but it works for me all the time."

Olsen gave another example of a time that he drew on help from the other side.

"My wife's older sister came down after a terrible divorce. She'd say her prayers, but she'd never been used to calling on someone from the other side to help her out.

"Well, she kept goats. I had to go to eastern Oregon to do a job, and while I was over there, I called back to check up on things and she said that the water had gone off in the well, so there was no water for her goats. I told her I couldn't get back until the next day, and she should call on her brother, Peter, to give her some help."

Since Peter was dead, she couldn't understand what Olsen meant. "How?" she asked.

"Just call for him and ask him." Olsen finally convinced her to give it a try, and she called on Peter to help her. The next time she tried the well, the water was back on. When she telephoned Olsen to let him know what happened, he said, "Well, I told you that if you ask, then they'll help you."

Funny thing is, the water only worked until Olsen's return. "When I got back the next day, the water was off again," Olsen said. "I found that the power was going down to the well, but there was no water coming out. So I went and got a new pump. When we started pulling up the old one, I said, 'I'll be darned.'"

Fifteen feet down from the surface, Olsen found a break in the electrical connection. The bottom end of the wires sagged back down into the well, only held up by a thin band of electrical tape.

"That pump couldn't have run," Olsen said. "The wires were burned in two. How that well got water, I don't know. Those kinds of things happen to me a lot. They kind of make you wonder sometimes."

Olsen got busy fastening the wires back together.

His sister-in-law watched him, her eyes wide with amazement. "How on earth did I get any water yesterday?" she asked.

Olsen shrugged and said, "You'll have to ask Peter."

Olsen shared another experience that he had with his brother.

"My brother was sixty-eight years old when he had his first heart attack. He made it through that one, so I went to see him and said, 'Kent, if you're going to check out of here, I want you to do some things for me.'"

Olsen asked his brother to take his love to their parents and also to their sister who'd been killed in a car accident. He also asked his brother to contact him if it was possible.

Kent gave his brother a bemused smile and answered, "I'll give it a shot."

Two months later, Kent suffered a second heart attack and went into a coma for about a week. "I don't know if he would have made it that time or not," Olsen said. "His kids voted to pull life support, and in five minutes, he was gone.

"It was about four days later and before the funeral when I was walking down the mall and I felt this pressure as though someone grabbed hold of me. I felt propelled into the Dalton bookstore and down a row of books. I was stopped right in front of a book called *Hello from Heaven.* I bought the book. It's not a religious book; it's about after death communications. The book had beautiful stories just full of love," Olsen said. "And I thought, 'Kent! It's you!' Then I thanked him.

"Twice more I knew it was him," Olsen said. "I was in another town about two weeks later, and I was working underneath a house. Kent and I were talking mind to mind and he gave me a message. His girls were fighting over his property. He had three girls and three boys. He told me that he and his ex-wife had agreed that everything he had would go to the boys, and everything she had would go to the girls.

"When I told his one boy what happened, he said that his girlfriend had been there at the time and heard them make that agreement."

Olsen says that spirits can also come to you in dreams.

"Kent had already been buried and he came to me in a dream. When he died, he was blind in one eye because he'd had diabetes, and his other eye was full of blood. He was gray haired and frail. In my dream, I felt him touch my arm and he said, 'Bryce, I can hear, I can see, I'm just fine.' I saw him, and he looked like he was twenty-five years old, with jet-black hair. He wasn't wearing his glasses.

"That sat me right up in bed and I knew he was there. I knew he was okay.

"This also lets you know how close we are to the other world," Olsen said. "You don't die. This body is a vehicle you go through this life with, and then you leave it. You are not your body. You're the life force in your body. You came by yourself and you leave by yourself."

Soft Landing

Who caught the three-year-old and set him on his feet?

Joni Bradley Richins scrubbed spaghetti sauce from the pan as she listened to her five children pound up the stairs to get their pajamas on. "Jessica and Candace!" Joni called after her two older daughters. "Help Rhett!"

Rhett, a spunky three-year-old, was wiser than his years. He learned through observing his four older siblings, as well as from his own daring exploits.

Joni rinsed the pan and set it upside down in the dish drainer. She wiped down the counters as she listened to thumps and bumps from the bedroom above the kitchen. It sounded like her children were playing instead of getting ready for bed. Rather than annoyance, Joni entertained a feeling of appreciation for the two-story house that she and her husband had bought several months before. Joni loved the added space of the upstairs bedrooms, but she hated it when her children popped the screen out from the bedroom window.

"The kids were told not to hang out the second story window and holler at their friends," Joni said, "But they kept doing it, even after we'd lived there several months. You'd think the novelty would wear off. They just kept popping the screen out. You know how kids are."

Joni pulled the plug in the sink and rinsed her dishcloth

under clear running water. She decided to go upstairs and get her children back on task as soon as she swept the floor.

Suddenly, her children's voices raised to shouts. Things were obviously getting out of hand. She'd have to go up now. She turned off the water. Then the chilling words from Candace's twin brother, Colten, reached her ears. "Mom! Rhett fell out the window!"

Horrifying images crowded into Joni's mind as she flung the dishcloth down and spun toward the outside door. "My heart seized with terror," Joni said. "If my-three-year old fell out a second story window onto a layer of sharp gravel, he could have two broken legs, or broken arms, or a concussion if he'd gone head first. Or worse."

Rhett's sister Kendra was five years old at the time. "I remember him sitting on the window sill and then he fell. It was scary," Kendra said.

Joni flew out the door and rounded the corner of the house, expecting to see blood and broken bones. "When I caught sight of Rhett, he was standing up, whimpering, and looking around as though he expected to see—or had just seen—somebody," Joni said. "I grabbed him up in my arms. The only wound I could find on his body was a tiny scratch on one ankle. As soon as I assured myself that he really was all right, I felt something, as though someone were there with us. I looked around, fully expecting to see someone standing there, but there was no one."

What are the odds that a toddler would fall two stories and land on his feet, with nothing but a small scratch? Joni believes that some ancestor from her husband's side of the family was watching over Rhett that day, and either carried him down and set him on his feet, or cushioned his fall.

"We own a field that belonged to Rhett's great-grandfather, and it has been in the family for four generations," Joni said. "I feel like it was someone from my husband's family that intervened, because if it had been my family, I would have felt a different closeness; but I still felt like it was family."

Joni's sensitivity to spirits can perhaps be traced to a time during her teenage years when she was quite ill. "I was lying on my bed in my room," Joni said. "All of a sudden, it was like I was out of my body, and I knew just what was going on in all parts of the house. I knew where each of my family members were and what they were doing." Before she could explore any further, her brother, Randy, found her lying on her bed. Her appearance frightened him so much that he yelled for their mother. "As soon as he started yelling, I was back in my body," Joni said.

In the case of her own children, sibling intervention wasn't helping any.

Joni wasn't willing to take any more chances that her children's guardian angels would always be there with arms outstretched, so she took matters into her own hands. "The very next morning, I went to town and bought security locks for all the windows."

Falling

Who stood by twelve-year-old Janna while she watched herself fall?

In March 1981, twelve-year-old Janna Lytle was helping baby-sit a group of young children whose mothers were playing an evening game of basketball. She and her adolescent friends, Kathy and Kristen, shepherded their charges into the upper hallway of the church building where the basketball game was underway. The old church was an architectural wonder, constructed of several levels so it would fit into the side of a hill. A cleverly designed assembly of ramps and stairs, bordered by a metal railing, led to the very top level.

"I was a typical kid," Janna said. "I thought it would be cool to slide down the railing."

The railing looked like solid brass, but when Janna impetuously threw her leg over it, it proved to be a brass sleeve over a metal rod. The sleeve was not fastened down, only held in place by caps at each end. It rolled easily under Janna's weight, her momentum tipping her over onto the opposite side of the stairs. Shocked at the unexpected twist of events, Janna couldn't hold on. She dropped toward the distant foyer floor.

That was when she had the strangest experience of her life.

"As soon as I tipped over, I was out of my body," Janna

said. "I stood below and watched my body tumble down through the air above me."

If that wasn't strange enough, Janna suddenly realized she wasn't alone. "I saw a large shoulder next to mine, on my right. I know it was a man. Whoever it was stood next to me, my shoulder touching his. He was wearing white."

Janna didn't see any more than his shoulder, perhaps due to the fact that a bright luminescence like she'd never seen before illuminated her falling body. The light funneled through the large southern-exposure window overlooking the staircase and foyer. Even though it was impossible at this hour of the evening, the window framed a light as bright as if the sun were close enough to knock. Janna's body tumbled down the outside edge of the window frame, her blonde hair shining as bright as broken spider web filament as it spun downward, flipping over and over, following her body's macabre acrobatics.

Janna doesn't remember her body hitting the floor. The next thing she knew, she woke up inside her body with sharp pain in her left arm and terrified voices screaming from above her. She blinked through a haze of blonde hair, then managed to shake the hair free of her face before she moaned in pain. She turned her head just enough to look up into the terrified face of Kathy standing far above her, looking over the railing that betrayed Janna's childish adventure and turned it into a horror story. As soon as Kathy saw Janna looking at her, Kathy's face disappeared from view.

Janna felt a sudden sense of panic. How could Kathy abandon her? She bunched her muscles in an effort to rise, but her body protested the slightest movement. Janna stared at the empty space where Kathy had stood seconds earlier. She felt totally alone, and longed for someone to be there, even someone as elusive as the man in white.

Before Janna could summon the energy to cry, Kristen's face appeared over the railing. "Kathy's gone for help," she called. "I'm keeping the kids away from the stairs."

Janna relaxed and closed her eyes.

"Are you okay?" Kristen yelled, her voice rising in panic.

Janna didn't have enough energy to answer.

Since Janna's backyard bordered the church property, her parents were at her side in almost no time.

"My dad said that my arm would feel better as soon as it stopped hurting," Janna remembers. "He was no help at all."

Janna's doctor happened to be her neighbor. He was given details of the accident before Janna's arrival at the hospital. Since he was familiar with the architecture of the church, when he heard how far she'd fallen, he prepared for the worst.

When Janna arrived, the doctor was stunned to see her walk into the room of her own power. He managed to mask his initial shock, but later told her mother what he was thinking.

"He told my mom he was amazed that I was even walking," Janna said. "Because of the distance of the fall, he expected at least a concussion, some major head trauma, and the very real possibility that I would be a vegetable for the rest of my life."

An examination showed that Janna's only injury was a broken left arm. The doctor set it in a cast, and Janna's parents took her home.

"I feel like I was protected by a guardian angel," Janna said. Then she gazed across the grass toward her two young adolescent sons. "Sometimes I wonder if it was one of my boys helping me."

Perhaps one day she'll find out who cushioned her fall, but until then, she's decided to leave off sliding down any railings that are more than one story high.

Hummingbird

Was the disoriented hummingbird connected to Grandma's fading life?

Darren Hansen turned toward the soft tap at his window, but with the morning sunlight slanting across the glass, he couldn't see anything. When he got up and moved across the room for a closer look, he was startled to see a frantic hummingbird bump against the window, then careen away on invisible wings.

Darren hurried outside to see the hummingbird flit in eccentric zigs and zags within the confines of the porch. "It had become disoriented for some reason," Darren said. "There were really just two walls to the porch, and the rest of it was open."

Shooing the bird toward an opening didn't work, since it seemed determined to escape through the window. "It was confused by a clear barrier that wouldn't allow it through," Darren said. "It wasn't trying to go the other way. I went inside the house and found an old plastic ice cream container. I quietly approached the hummingbird and placed the container over it, then carefully slipped a piece of hard paper between it and the window, trapping the bird inside. I walked out of the open porch area and released it."

The next spring, the bird was back. "It came not once, but a few times, and each time I happened to be at home and released it. I was concerned because we were moving soon and I figured that someone else might not help it out. I was also confused why the hummingbird kept returning to this place."

Darren couldn't help but notice a correlation between the confused hummingbird and his grandmother. "It was interesting to look at the fact that Grandma had become a victim of Alzheimer's and was also very disoriented as a person. My family had to watch out for her and help her."

As spring aged into summer, the hummingbird stopped visiting the Hansen's house. In the fall, Darren and his family moved a half-mile away, across town. Darren all but forgot about the hummingbird.

But the hummingbird hadn't forgotten Darren.

One afternoon, his children called him at work to say that there was a hummingbird in the garage. Even though the garage door was wide open, they couldn't get the hummingbird to go out. Darren couldn't leave work to go home, so it was a few hours before he could help.

"I discovered the hummingbird in a very weak condition in our garage, barely able to move," Darren said. "At first I thought it was dead, but when I tried to pick it up, I found there was life in it because it tried to resist my help. I felt that it was the same bird."

Darren tenderly helped the little bird out of the garage and placed it in a patch of soft grass underneath a tree. He didn't have any misconceptions that the little bird would survive, but he wanted to give it a peaceful place to die.

"The following day I received a phone call telling me that my grandmother had passed away," Darren said. "I felt that the two were related, but I can give no real explanation. Perhaps this bird was a symbol of my grandmother's weakening condition; perhaps the hummingbird was her favorite type of bird. I don't know."

Since Grandma's funeral, the Hansens have not seen a single hummingbird near their house.

Seeing Grandpa

The toddler recognized his grandpa's picture taken forty years earlier.

Seven-month-old Alex opened his mouth and leaned forward for another bite of macaroni and cheese. "Good boy," his mother, Anna, said. Alex grinned, showing his toothless gums. He banged his spoon against his high chair tray.

"Do you want a drink?" Anna asked.

Alex banged again.

Anna got up and went over to fridge for the apple juice. She filled Alex's sippy cup, then turned around to see a strange sight.

Alex was twisted sideways in his chair, holding his little spoon up in the air. "He was saying, 'Grandpa, some? Grandpa, some?'" Anna said. "I asked, 'What are you doing?'"

Alex turned toward his mother, his face alight with joy. "Grandpa!" he said.

"He kept smiling and waving at the same spot beside him," Anna said.

Before Anna could ask any more questions, the telephone rang. She picked it up, her gaze fixed on her son, who had turned back to wave his spoon in the air, still babbling about Grandpa.

"Hello?" Anna said into the receiver.

"Oh, Anna," her husband said from the other end of the

line, his voice thick with emotion. "Dad just died."

Anna was stunned to silence. They had visited her in-laws only three weeks earlier, with no sign whatsoever that anything was wrong. Her father-in-law was only fifty-seven years old.

Anna found her voice and did her best to console her husband over the phone. After she hung up, she turned to stare at her son.

"I got goose bumps," Anna said. "I didn't feel anything scary; it was just strange. I knew that Alex was talking to someone else in the room."

A few days later, Anna and her family were back at her in-laws for a more somber visit. With a house full of mourners, Anna tucked Alex into her arms and wandered down a hallway lined with family portraits that she'd never taken the time to examine before. She stopped to study her husband's high school graduation picture when Alex suddenly strained against her grasp.

"Grandpa!" he cried, reaching toward the photograph of an unfamiliar young man of eighteen or nineteen.

"Alex! Hold still!" Anna said, getting a better grip on the squirming child.

"Grandpa!" Alex insisted, waving his little hands at the portrait.

When Anna moved closer to the picture, she realized with a sudden start that this could be her father-in-law in his younger days. Later on, she confirmed her suspicion with her mother-in-law.

"I wouldn't have recognized him," Anna said. "But my son knew what his grandpa looked like when he was younger. I think kids, especially little kids, are able to see the other side."

Angel in a Car

Sometimes we just need to realize we are loved.

Ken Williams had never felt so useless in his life. He stumbled along the dirt road, his eyes blurred with tears, not caring where he was going or how far he wandered from town. It wouldn't even matter if he died out here on this dirt track that saw hardly a single car all day. There was no one at home waiting for him, no one to care if he ever got back at all. His wife had left him. Instead of feeling peace at the absence of her increasing dissatisfaction, he felt utterly rejected. If his wife couldn't love him, then who could?

If that wasn't bad enough, he was a failure at work, too. He'd been let go from his job, leaving his days achingly empty.

Ken raised his face to the sky, a slight breeze cooling the tears on his cheeks. "God!" Ken screamed. "Are you there? Or do You hate me too?"

He waited, gulping in air, trying to stifle his sobs. The breeze lifted his hair and set it back again, as though trying to soothe him. Ken grabbed his hair with both fists and screamed, "One thing would have been bad enough! But I can't survive this pain, I can't survive, I can't! Where are You, God? Where are You?"

The silence that followed his desperate outburst was heavy, pushing Ken's heart even deeper into despair. He dropped his hands, slumped his shoulders, and with his eyes fixed on the dirt at his feet, he trudged onward.

It took a moment for Ken to register the humming sound of an approaching car. He turned his head away and walked as close to the edge of the road as he could. To his dismay, the engine slowed and then idled at the spot right next to him.

The last thing Ken wanted right now was to talk to anyone. He slowly turned his head and stared at the car with undisguised irritation.

"Excuse me, sir," said the young woman behind the wheel. "Could you please tell me which way I need to go to get to town?"

Ken glanced ahead and saw that he had nearly reached a junction with a four way stop. Although he didn't feel like helping anyone, the fastest way to get rid of the motorist was to give her directions. "I told her to take a left at the stop sign, go about a mile and a half along the straight stretch of road, and then turn left again. That would take her back to town."

The woman thanked Ken, then pulled a few feet forward to the stop sign and began turning left. Suddenly, her brake lights went on, and she leaned out of her window. "Sir? Sir?" she called.

"All I wanted was to be rid of the nuisance, to be able to go on with my crying, to sit on my pity pot, and be left alone," Ken said. "So I answered her rather harshly."

The woman was unfazed. She smiled brightly and said "Jesus loves you," then pushed the accelerator.

A spark of hope kindled in Ken's heart. "I looked up into the sky in disbelief," Ken said. "Then I dropped my gaze and looked down the road."

There was no car in sight.

Startled, Ken made a dash for the intersection, checking each road that led to it, even glancing back along the one he'd been traveling.

Nothing.

There was no way the driver could have gotten out of view in such a short time, not even if she'd been going a hundred miles an hour. She couldn't have plunged off the road out of sight, since the shoulders were all flat. The woman and her car had simply vanished.

"I truly believe that I experienced a visit from an angel of God," Ken said.

With fresh tears of gratitude, Ken made his way back to town and the beginning of a new life.

Part 2

Devils, Demons, and Scary Things

The Devil's Calling

Some things may be right for one person but not another.

Never doubt that the devil knows what's what and will try to steer you wrong every single time.

But Jesus, well, He'll tell you what's right and help you if you ask Him. Every single time.

Jeff knows all of this firsthand, because he's been around both of them, so close in fact, that the devil spoke right in his ear.

Trying to make sense of his beloved stepfather's death when he was just a teenager, Jeff tried to figure out what he was supposed to do with the rest of his life. He thought that maybe he should be a preacher.

Preaching might be just fine for some people. But from where Jeff now stands at the sunset end of his life, he knows without a doubt that it wouldn't have been the right path for him.

Which is exactly the reason the devil wanted him to take it.

Wrestling with his decision prompted Jeff to seek out different church men for advice. "They all told me the same story," Jeff said. "I had to be called of God. When I asked them how I would know when God called me, they all said I would just know. I believed in God with all my heart. I honestly wanted to become a preacher because I thought that was the best way to serve Him. But I didn't know about the issue of 'being called.'

"Nothing special happened to me, other than just wanting to become a preacher. When I asked other preachers to clarify the calling part, they tried to tell me I'd been called. It didn't compute. I didn't recognize anything in my life that could constitute a call.

"They made light of me and said I was looking for something more than God was willing to give. Through it all, I felt I needed to know for sure within myself when the call came."

While for some people one religion is as good as another, for Jeff, the specific teachings of a church really mattered.

"I suppose old Scratch knew if he could get me to be a preacher, it would make it more difficult for me to accept the true gospel when the time came for me to hear it. That time was still a few years down the road yet.

"This event happened one morning. It had to be Saturday, because I was in no hurry to get out of bed. I'd been awake for several minutes, thinking things over. Suddenly, I felt something very strange happening to me. I tingled from head to toe, and became paralyzed to the point I couldn't move so much as a finger as a dark, cold feeling settled over me.

"I lay there for several seconds, knowing something was about to happen but not knowing what.

"Then it happened. I heard a voice in a loud whisper with my natural ears, just as clearly as I've ever heard anything or anyone in my life before or since. One word was spoken, and it was spoken twice. I can still hear it in my mind to this day. It said, 'PREACHER! PREACHER!'

"I lay paralyzed for several more seconds. Then it let up, and I was left alone."

The only thing young Jeff could surmise from this experience was that he had been called. Yet for some reason, he never followed through on the calling. It could have been because he was a busy teenager, or maybe it was the residual unease from the paralysis, darkness, and cold that preceded the "calling." Whatever it was, Jeff is grateful that he didn't follow through with this unsettling prompting. "In the light of what I know now, I know I was in the presence of Satan," Jeff said. "It was a cold feeling, the coldest feeling I've ever felt, void of anything spiritual. And where the Spirit of the Lord speaks to us spirit to spirit, this person spoke to me with words I could hear in my ears."

It was several years later when Jeff found himself on the opposite end of the spiritual spectrum. This time, he sat with his wife, Doreen, in a place that was very sacred to them.

"While seated there, I became aware of a presence in the room that drew my full attention. I knew someone was there, though I could see no one. I knew the exact spot where the person stood, at the end of the room, just to the right of a mirror. I had the strongest feeling that this person was extremely righteous. I sat, just looking at the place for a very long time. The feeling of peace and love that radiated toward me with a magnetic-like pull from that spot left no doubt someone was there.

"When we left, Doreen and I decided to go across the street to an ice cream place and have banana splits. We did that on some of our first dates, and with our anniversary just three days away, we felt like celebrating."

As Jeff and Doreen sat in the car with their treats, Doreen told Jeff that she'd felt like they'd just been in the presence of someone very righteous. As they compared their impressions, they found that their stories matched in the smallest detail, even to the exact location of the person.

A month later, through a special blessing given by the power of God, it was revealed to Jeff and Doreen that it was Jesus Christ himself whom they had been in the presence of in that sacred place.

"Had I known at the time that the person was Jesus Christ, I probably would have hurried out of the room, feeling unworthy to be in His presence," Jeff said. "Yet that was the most spiritual experience I've ever enjoyed in my life."

Lightning from Nowhere

Evil spirits wait for an invitation.

Jennifer lived in Salt Lake City with her husband, Dave, and two-year-old son, Jared. She liked her job, and enjoyed working with her good friend, Beth Ann. She got along with her other coworkers, too, until Adelaide was hired.

From their first meeting, Jennifer was uncomfortable around Adelaide, even though her feelings made no sense. Adelaide was well groomed, had a ready smile, and didn't chew with her mouth open, yet Jennifer just couldn't seem to relax around her. She found herself avoiding her.

One day, she tried talking with Beth Ann to see if she had the same feelings, but Beth Ann thought that Adelaide was fascinating.

You're just being silly, Jennifer chided herself. *You need to get over it. Just be friends.* Yet she could never quite talk herself into getting any closer to Adelaide.

One day, the two women ended up stocking shelves side by side. Jennifer forced herself to work beside Adelaide, even though something inside urged her to make some excuse to get away.

Adelaide began asking questions. "How long have you worked here?" "How big is the family you came from?" "What's your birth order?"

Jennifer gave vague and guarded answers.

"How many children do you have?" "Are you having more?" "How long have you been married?" "Who's your husband?"

As the questions became more personal, Jennifer grew more uncomfortable. Finally, she turned the tables. "Adelaide, what do you want to be when you grow up?" she asked with a playful smile that she really didn't mean.

"Oh," Adelaide answered, "I want to teach people astral travel."

"Astral travel?" as soon as the question was out, Jennifer wished she could take it back.

Adelaide nodded, her eyes shining. "Well, it's like, your ordinary, everyday séance is so archaic. It's much more effective to mingle spirit to spirit." Adelaide gave Jennifer a meaningful glance. "I should know."

"You…?" Jennifer couldn't find the words to finish her question.

"That's just the first step," Adelaide said, her gaze narrowing as she smiled with dark and subtle knowing. She leaned closer, and Jennifer drew back. "The unseen ones want to be part of our lives. The power they have is thrilling; they know things that you couldn't even guess."

Jennifer's hands trembled as she pushed product onto the shelves, doing her best to avoid her coworker's eye. But when Adelaide let out a loud, eerie laugh, Jennifer glanced over. What she saw made her nearly drop the box clutched in her hand.

Her frightened gaze fastened on a disembodied face above Adelaide's head, a dark visage with distorted features that resembled a sly, cruel fox face.

"I've got to go," Jennifer squeaked, then turned and fled.

Using the experience as a warning, Jennifer no longer felt guilty for avoiding Adelaide.

A week later, Jennifer discovered she was pregnant. She and David rejoiced, agreeing to keep the news to themselves for the time being. Jennifer couldn't wait to pull out the box of old baby clothes that Jared had outgrown. With Jared's help, she riffled through the tiny outfits.

The next day, she went to work with a light heart, greeting Beth Ann with a warm smile.

"Nice to see you so cheerful," Beth Ann said. "Lately you've been walking around like you had a storm cloud parked over your head."

A momentary chill slid down Jennifer's back like an ice cube on a warm ironing board. Then she straightened up and said, "I'm better now." She really wanted to share the news about her coming baby with her friend, but it was still so early in the pregnancy that a lot could go wrong. She and Dave had decided to wait at least a month to tell anyone, and she would stick to it.

Halfway through her workday, Jennifer noticed Adelaide at a table in the lunchroom shuffling a stack of cards. Jennifer averted her eyes.

"Jennifer," Adelaide called. "Let me read your cards."

Jennifer shook her head.

"You'd be surprised what you could find out about yourself."

Not bothering to reply, Jennifer left to eat her lunch elsewhere. By the time she finished her sandwich, she needed a drink. She headed for the vending machine in the hall, but when she got there, she couldn't find her money in her pocket. She went back to the lunchroom to see if she'd dropped it there.

Adelaide still sat at the table. Beth Ann was at her side, her hand turned up as Adelaide's fingers spidered their way across her palm. Jennifer wanted to warn Beth Ann not to have anything to do with Adelaide, but it would just be a waste of breath, so she concentrated on passing in and out of the lunchroom unnoticed.

"You have a short, dark haired friend who is pregnant," Adelaide said, each word loud and clear.

Jennifer's heart began pumping ice water.

"There is something wrong with her baby," Adelaide said.

She wasn't reading Beth Ann's palm... she was telling Jennifer things she didn't want to know. Jennifer fled the lunchroom, the lost money insignificant.

A month and a half later, Jennifer looked into the solemn face of her doctor.

"You must go on bed rest if you want to keep this baby," the doctor intoned, his eyebrows drawing together for emphasis.

It was easy to say but hard to do with an active little boy who'd just turned three. Dave tried to help when he was home, but after a week of him hovering around, it was almost harder on Jennifer than if he were gone.

At the end of the week, Dave's brother, John, and his wife, Emily, came over with a casserole. While the women visited in the bedroom, Jennifer overheard John ask if Dave wanted to go duck hunting with him that weekend.

"I can't," Dave answered.

"It's all right, Dave, you go ahead," Jennifer called.

"Jennifer?" She heard footsteps in the hallway, and then Dave appeared at the door. "I can't just leave you here alone."

Jennifer waved her hand. "Of course you can. You hunt ducks early in the morning, right? Jared and I will be sleeping most of the time. We'll be just fine, and besides, you need a break."

"Are you sure?"

"I'm sure."

So it was arranged.

Early Saturday morning, while it was still full dark, Jennifer was startled awake by a crash, followed by the splintering sound of a breaking dish. Dave must have dropped a plate in the kitchen down the hall, but before she could ask if everything was all right, she heard more crashes in quick succession.

"Help!" a little boy cried, his small voice pitiful. "Help me!"

"Jared!" Jennifer called in alarm. She pushed back her covers and swung her legs over the side of the bed. Pressing her hand against the baby that hung tenaciously to a fragile thread of life within her, she stumbled into the hallway, heading for the kitchen where the crash of breaking dishes continued.

Where was Dave? What was Jared doing in the kitchen? He couldn't reach the dishes in the cupboard. She wondered if he'd climbed on a chair. She had to help him, but before she reached the kitchen doorway, a calm voice said, "Go back to bed."

Jennifer stopped and glanced around in confusion. Who had spoken? They must be very near, but she saw no one. A few more steps, and Jennifer would be able to see what was causing all the commotion.

The voice sounded a second time. "I was told to turn around and get back in bed, and that everything was fine," Jennifer said.

Filled with a sudden, inexplicable peace, Jennifer obeyed the voice and went back into her room, in spite of not knowing what was going on in her kitchen.

Before sliding back into the nest of covers still warm from her body, Jennifer saw that Jared was snuggled on Dave's side of the bed, sound asleep. Dave must have put him there before he left.

Jennifer curled herself around her son and drifted off to sleep despite the background of splintering crashes coming down the hall.

In the morning, the kitchen was just as clean as it had been the night before, with not a single sliver of glass in sight.

Jennifer slept right through the next unusual event, but her neighbor, Vicky, didn't. One morning Vicky walked into Jennifer's bedroom, put her hands on her hips, and said,

"What was going on here last night?"

Jennifer thought back over the previous evening. After bringing her supper, Dave cleaned the kitchen, read Jared a story, and put him to bed. Then he climbed under the covers beside Jennifer.

"Is everything all right?" Jennifer had asked.

"Yeah, sure. Why?"

Jennifer shrugged. "I don't know. I just feel restless."

"Well, honey, it's no wonder, you've been down for quite awhile."

"Yeah." Jennifer stared at the ceiling while Dave rolled over and pulled the covers up to his ears.

"Did you lock the doors?" she asked.

"Yes."

Jennifer stared into the gloom of the darkened room.

"Did Jared brush his teeth?"

"Yes," Dave said. "Everything's fine. Now go to sleep."

Jennifer finally slept.

Now Jennifer faced Vicky's curious question with a blank stare. "Nothing happened last night."

Vicky leaned closer and said, "Then what was that lightning in your basement?"

Jennifer blinked in surprise. "Lightning? In my *house?*"

Vicky raised her hands in her own defense. "Yes! Lights were flashing all over the place, from one side of your basement to the other! Harry saw it too! You can ask him!"

The hair on Jennifer's arms crawled to a standing position. "Lightning in my house," she whispered.

Vicky nodded. "I thought you were having a party or something, but I couldn't imagine that you'd do that in your condition." Vicky's gaze traveled to Jennifer's midsection.

Jennifer slid her hands over her belly, her heart beating in agitation as she tried to make sense of what she'd just heard.

When Dave got home from work, he checked the

basement, but there was no evidence of lightning having raged through it.

Eventually, Jennifer's baby, Brad, was born early. His underdeveloped lungs resulted in a life-flight to a pediatric hospital. Yet after all was said and done, Brad turned out to be all right.

"I think it all goes back to Adelaide," Jennifer said. "Knowing her was the only thing that was different between having Jared and having Brad. I think it was because I wouldn't let her get to me that nothing really bad could happen. Like when I heard the crashing, I thought there was something wrong, but it came to me to relax and not go down the hallway. I was being protected. Then when I saw Jared safely asleep in my bed, I could sleep too.

"You can be protected if you're doing what you're supposed to. I think if I had let Adelaide read my cards or my palm, then it would have been worse, because I would have been inviting the evil thing in. I think I was shown that evil face for a warning.

"I found out later that Adelaide had split personalities and she was in cults and things. I was afraid to have her around my kids. My friend Beth Ann still hung around her, but I said no, I wouldn't have her by me or my kids. I just wouldn't."

In the Dark

Did this spirit spring from a murder or a séance?

"Hey, Janet, I'll be off my shift in ten minutes. Let me drive you home."

Janet lifted her head and brushed her soft brown hair to one side. "Yeah, sure, Joe," she told the bartender.

That was the last time he ever saw her.

Police investigators determined that Janet had returned to her apartment, changed clothes, and gone out again, leaving her purse behind. There were no signs of forced entry or a struggle. They told Janet's family that they would do everything they could to find the missing young woman.

Several days later, Janet's battered body was discovered in a remote area.

For a time, the family suspected that she'd been abducted by the infamous murderer Ted Bundy, yet investigators officially ruled him out.

"They told us it definitely wasn't Bundy," Janet's younger sister, Darla, said. "Before, when I thought it was some psycho guy, it was like water under the bridge. But now, thinking that it might be someone you know, that makes it really awful."

Darla was only eleven years old when her sister died. After that, she always made sure that her little dog was in her room before she'd go to sleep. She'd avoid looking at

Janet's high school graduation picture in the hallway, an old black and white with Janet's sparkling brown eyes looking out of the frame in optimistic anticipation of her future. It had been brushed with colored pencils by the photographer of the era, giving Janet a slight blush to her cheeks and a tinge of red to her lips.

Darla soon convinced her parents to move Janet's picture into their bedroom. They hung it on their wall opposite the open door, so that Janet's eyes stared out into the hallway.

One day, Darla's mother stopped her in the hall to ask, "Darla, have you noticed anything strange lately?"

"Strange? How?"

"Well, I don't quite know how to say it."

"Just say it, Mom."

Darla's mother searched the ceiling for a moment, then looked back down. "Well, it's just that sometimes, it seems like I feel… I don't know… it's like someone sits on the edge of my bed in the night, when it's dark." She watched Darla's eyes, waiting for a reaction.

"Maybe it's Dad."

Her mother shook her head. "It happens when Dad's asleep next to me."

"Well, then, who does it look like?"

"I never see anyone. It's always dark."

A chill danced along Darla's spine.

"I don't think it's anything to worry about," Mom assured her. "I just wondered… that if it happened to you too… then maybe it's Janet coming back to visit." Mom's voice faded to a whisper.

"I haven't felt anything," Darla said.

Those words came back to haunt her, because within the week, Darla woke up in the dark of night to feel something press down the edge of her bed with enough pressure to shift her weight slightly, exactly as it would if her mother or father had sat down by her.

Darla stared around her room. There was no one else to

be seen in the dim interior, even though she could make out the vague shapes of her dresser and closet door and hear her dog's quiet breathing as it slept on the floor beside her. The only thing visible on the bed was the shadowy outline of her own body shrouded in blankets, her toes tipped toward whatever it was that had plopped itself next to her.

Darla tried to swallow with a throat sucked dry by fear. "Janet?" she whispered. "Is that you?"

There was no reply.

The utility room door in Darla's childhood home happened to be straight across the hall from her parent's bedroom. One night when Darla was in her teens, she was home alone. As she walked down the hall, she averted her eyes from Janet's photograph, glancing into the utility room, as usual. But she didn't see what she usually saw. "I saw a shadowy figure move past the doorway."

The sight jolted her into action. With hair standing on end and limbs tingling, she dashed outside and high-tailed it to the neighbor's house, her dog hard on her heels. They stayed there until her parents got home.

"Dad didn't believe that there was anything wrong, but Mom did. She said that sometimes when she was in the bathroom, someone would try to get in. She'd watch the locks turn and the door would open, but there would be no one there."

When Darla was nearly eighteen years old, she was dozing off one night and dreamed about being at the mall with someone standing beside her. When the clock chimed ten o'clock PM, she woke up and saw a dark shadow by her bed. She made a dash for her parent's room, but before she could reach it, she was knocked to the floor. Her dog was going nuts, barking non-stop.

"Whenever I felt something sitting on my bed before, I used to think it really was Janet coming back," Darla said. "I hoped that maybe she was going to find a way to tell me who it was that killed her. But this was definitely not Janet coming back for a visit. When it flattened me, I thought, *this is not Janet.* There was no way it was her."

Darla's mother opened the door of her bedroom. "Darla?"

The black shape disappeared. The dog calmed down and trotted over to Darla's side, waiting while Darla got to her feet and dashed into her mother's arms.

Darla never found out what the dark shadow was.

"I wonder if the way Janet died brought something bad into the house," Darla said. "Or maybe it had something to do with a séance that I went to when I was just a kid. I was only in fifth or sixth grade, and a bunch of us girls were having a sleepover and we sat around a card table and held hands and tried to talk to somebody, but we didn't know what we were doing. Nothing happened there."

But strange and frightening things most certainly happened afterward, things that remain just as mysterious to this day as the identity of Janet's killer.

The Shadow

Once seen by the father, once by his son; is the family being stalked?

David Barney shouldered his way to the bathroom sink, crowding in next to his friend, Roger. David had the narrow neck of a pink balloon stretched as wide as his ten-year-old fingers could get it.

"Hey!" Roger, shouted as he tried to re-fit the mouth of his balloon over the bathroom faucet. "It's my turn!"

"But Brenda just came outside!" David said, ducking around his friend to check the side yard, visible from the bathroom window. "I've got to smack her with a water balloon!" Brenda had just moved to Richfield, Utah, and David was anxious to make an impression on her.

"If you can't wait, then go use the kitchen sink," Roger said, squeezing his hand around the neck of his balloon that was now snug up around the water spigot. He twisted the sink handle with a slow and careful hand until the blue balloon began to swell like a frog getting ready to croak.

"But your mom's in there!" David protested.

Not only was Roger's mother using the kitchen sink, but David didn't know if she'd actually approve of her son's friend smacking little girls in the head with water balloons. Sometimes moms didn't understand about having fun.

"Okay, I'm done," Roger said, easing the lips of his bloated balloon off the faucet.

David darted another look out the window to check on

Brenda's position. What he saw made him forget all about Brenda, all about Roger's mom, and even the balloon that sagged in his suddenly petrified fingers. In spite of it being the middle of the summer of 1970, prickles of cold danced along the back of David's neck as he stared at what couldn't possibly be.

"Roger," David whispered.

"What?" Roger struggled to tie his balloon shut.

"Roger!" David said, nudging his friend's arm with his elbow. The blue balloon slipped and sputtered as it rolled over in the sink, spewing water on the counter like clear blood as it writhed in a miniature death throe.

"Aw, what'd you do that for?" Roger complained. "I almost had it!"

"Look," David said, not taking his eyes from the window. "Do you see that?"

Roger looked up, a frown of annoyance on his face. When he saw what David pointed at, his eyebrows shot up and his eyes popped out.

A shadow streaked the grass in Roger's side yard like the long swipe of a muddy shoe. It began at a point on the ground just six feet from the window the boys stared through, stretching across the grass with its long, narrow legs, and folding itself up along the side of the house into a torso. Just above that, the shadow ended with a head. It was the shadow of a man, no mistake about that, but something was dreadfully wrong. There was no one standing outside. At least, no one the boys could see. Where one would expect to see the shadow intersect with the feet of the person it belonged to, was a patch of grass, glaringly empty. Yet something had to be there to cast the shadow. And whatever it was stood directly in front of the window, looking in at them.

As soon as David realized that some unseen being could be staring at him as intently as he was watching the shadow, a shiver of dread shot through him, shaking the empty balloon from his fingers. He didn't even notice it fall to the floor. Every hair on his ten-year-old body stood out in sudden fright. It was hard to breathe, as though the shadow were crawling in through his nostrils and filling his open mouth, sliding down into his pulsing lungs, squeezing the air and the life right out of him.

Roger gasped as though he'd just been struck with the same terror. David turned and looked at Roger in the very instant that Roger turned to look at him. Roger's horrified face scared David as much as the thought of a sinister ghost measuring them with invisible eyes.

As one, the boys turned and fled the bathroom, heading for the kitchen and Roger's mother.

"Mom, Mom, Mom! There's a shadow out the window; come on, you've got to see!" Roger shouted, barreling into the kitchen and nearly colliding with his startled mother. David, glued to his side, bumped into Roger when he braked to a sudden stop.

"Roger, calm down," his mother said, obviously not grasping the seriousness of the situation. "What did you see?"

"A shadow, only there's no one there!" Roger shouted, grabbing his mother's hand and pulling her toward the bathroom.

To her credit, Roger's mother didn't protest and allowed herself to be led along. Roger stopped in front of the window, his eyes searching the ground. "It's gone," he said. Then he whirled to face David. "But it was there, wasn't it?"

David's eyes took in the sun-soaked grass. His gaze crawled up the wall that the shadow had darkened only moments before, but now was bathed in sunlight.

"Yeah, I saw it, honest, it was a shadow like someone was standing right there, but nobody was," David said.

"Hm," Roger's mom said. "Well, there's nothing out there now, but I see that you boys made a mess in here." She pointed to the water on the counter. It had pooled to the edge and made a steady *drip, drip, drip* onto the floor. "Clean it up."

"But, Mom!" Roger said.

"If you make a mess, clean it up, or no more water balloons," Roger's mom said. Then she headed back to the kitchen.

David stared out the window again, fearful that the shadow would return as soon as Roger's mother was gone. It turned out that he didn't need to worry about that until years later.

In July 2005, David stepped outside of his house and saw his son, seventeen-year-old Trevor, talking on his cell phone as he climbed into his truck. Deciding to speak to his son later, David gave his son a single wave of dismissal and turned to go back inside.

Just then, Trevor let out a yelp of alarm.

David turned to see Trevor staring at the ground, his cell phone pulled away from his ear, his phone call forgotten.

"Did you see that?" Trevor asked, pointing.

"See what?" David asked, moving off the porch and searching the ground as he moved toward his son.

"That shadow!"

"What shadow?"

"The one by my truck, like some guy was standing there!"

In his excitement, Trevor sounded as though he was accusing his dad of mischief, but David had been on the porch fifteen feet away when Trevor spotted the body-less shadow of a man that was gone by the time David reached his son's side.

David told Trevor his childhood story of a frightening encounter with a shadow that had no body. Trevor didn't seem to be in any hurry to get back to his truck as he considered his father's words. After a thoughtful pause, he said, "Hey, Dad, maybe you've got a shadow stalking you."

His son's words sent icy fingers tapping their way up David's back, reminding him that he wasn't in the habit of looking back to see who... or what... might be following him.

Fighting the Devil

There's a right way and a wrong way to make him leave.

In the late summer of 1988, while the nights grew chill and the sun died a little earlier each evening, Hannah Good decided it was time to make a change in her lifestyle. "I decided to fix all the screw-ups in my life," she said. She determined that she was going to church and that she'd end all the bad habits she had.

Shortly after Hannah began taking concrete steps in this new life direction, she went to bed one night feeling like she was really and truly on top of things. That was when she met the devil.

"Some people say it was just a dream," Hannah said. "But it was no dream. It was real."

Hannah was somewhat startled to see an incredibly handsome man sitting on the edge of her bed. His muscular body was clad all in black, and his broad shoulders filled out the dark coat he wore. His black hair was combed, his intense black eyes were fixed on her, and he had a heart-stopping chiseled jaw that would put any movie star to shame. He was the best looking guy Hannah had ever seen, but that didn't give him any right to be in her bedroom.

"Who are you?" Hannah demanded. As soon as the words left her mouth, she knew exactly who he was. The devil stared back at her, completely at ease in her presence.

Hannah's heart beat faster. "What are you doing here?"

He continued to stare at her, a hint of amusement in his dark eyes.

Hannah's heart began thudding against her ribcage so hard it hurt.

"You need to leave," Hannah declared, her voice coming out braver than she felt.

The man blinked languidly, as though she hadn't spoken at all.

"I know who you are," Hannah said, her voice rising in panic. "Get out of here."

He still didn't bother to answer, but kept watching Hannah with dark amusement as she became more and more agitated.

"Leave!" Hannah shouted, pointing toward the door.

This time the man opened his perfect mouth and said in a deep bass voice that rolled out as smooth as oil on a tropical sea, "You'll never change. You'll always be the same."

Hannah froze at the sound of his hypnotic voice.

He gave her a striking half-smile that showed straight, white, even teeth, and continued, "You might as well commit your soul to me now."

Hannah suddenly found her voice and yelled, "No! Get out!"

He shook his head slightly in mock regret. "Well, then, I'll just have to take one of your kids. Which one do you want to part with?" His smirk slipped into a wicked smile.

Hannah's heart felt like it had stopped beating. No one was taking any of her kids anywhere, and to even threaten it was asking for trouble. "I was so mad, I pulled back my fist and punched him in the jaw," Hannah said.

Instead of getting angry, the devil started to laugh.

"I can still hear the laugh to this day," Hannah said, her voice quiet. "It was pure, pure, evil. Bad, bad news."

In an instant, the man's face changed from an icon of masculine perfection to a face of evil so twisted, it was hard for Hannah to even look at. "I got really scared. The only thing I could think of was what I'd learned in the few times I hadn't sluffed my religion class. I began saying, 'In the name of Jesus Christ I command you to leave, in the name of Jesus Christ I command you to leave,' over and over as fast as I could."

Where all of her earlier demands had been ignored, this one got results. "I just kept saying it as fast as it came out of my mouth, and he just kind of dissipated, like smoke—not fog—but like smoke that went away."

Shuddering with a curious mixture of relief and revulsion, Hannah closed her eyes. When she opened them, she was staring up at her ceiling, with a cold draft of air moving across her face, in spite of the closed bedroom windows. "I didn't have the air conditioner or a swamp cooler on," she said. "It was cold on my cheek, just like someone was standing at my side and blowing air across my face to the left. It was so eerie. I was freezing, even though I was under the covers."

After a moment of thought, Hannah said quietly, "I think it was because I was such a good follower of the bad guy that he came to me like that." She gave a wry laugh. "I'd sluffed half of school and half of my religion class, but there was that one thing I remembered when I needed it. Even though I was trying to clean up my act, I think I was still vulnerable. He figured if he could get me right then, he wouldn't have to fight for me so much later." She shook her head. "He had me for all those years and he didn't have to work very hard to keep me, either. I always lived on the wild side of life, not as wild as everyone thought, but I was a pretty sure bet. When I had this change of heart, he figured if he got me at the crossroads, then I'd go back." She looked down at her hands. "I did for awhile, too."

Then she raised her head and sat a little straighter. "But this time I'm determined to stick with what I know is right, even though I'm fully expecting another visit before too long."

Haunted House

The old house once belonged to a doctor;
now it is occupied by ghosts.

Gail Walker's first night in her new house was spent camped on the family room floor with her four daughters and her sister and brother-in-law, Dee and Dan Gibbens. The Victorian-era Queen Anne style house was admittedly run-down, but it was also magnificent, with a basement, two stories, and an attic. Built by John Dorius, Jr., in 1897, it had originally served as the town's first library, and then was used by a local doctor as his residence and medical clinic. Artists would often sit across the street, gazing at the gingerbread trim and carefully sketching the contours of the roof, the windows, and the wide, wrap-around porch, taking pains to get the unusual turret window in the roof just right.

"I woke up the day after we got there to hear my five-year-old daughter talking in the front foyer," Gail said. "I asked, 'Who is Heather out there talking to?'"

No one knew, so the family went to investigate.

"Heather was sitting alone on the steps. I said, 'Heather who are you talking to?'

"'My dad,' she said. But her father had passed away the year before."

Heather told her mother that she was actually sitting on her daddy's lap, and that he was in heaven where it was very pretty, everybody wore white, and the flowers were lovely.

She assured her mother that Daddy was very happy.

"She told me that my husband got to watch over some children," Gail said. "He told her that he loved our farm and the beautiful flowers around it." This makes sense, because even though the house is nearly in the center of town, there's an old barn standing behind it.

That unusual incident was only the beginning.

While the Walkers set up beds and dressers in their bedrooms and became accustomed to the floor plan, the family's black cat, Midnight, did not.

"He was a normal cat until we moved there," said Gail's oldest child, Barbie Walker Stewart, who was fifteen years old when they moved to the house in 1981. "Then he became really jumpy. He'd run up and down the stairs, and spit and scratch for no reason. He was never the same after we moved to that house." The cat's actions became so bizarre that Gail decided it was best to have him put to sleep.

The current owners, Paul and Jackie Richardson, moved into the house in August 2005. In May 2006, Paul got up at 4:30 AM and was in the kitchen when he heard Jackie walking down the same staircase that had seemed to drive the Walker's cat ballistic. When Jackie didn't join him, Paul called, "Jackie?" He got no answer, so he moved to the bottom of the stairs and called again, waking Jackie up in their bedroom on the second floor. Then he realized the footsteps couldn't have been hers.

The Richardsons' guests also had strange encounters. Their friends, Sam and Laura, came to visit at Thanksgiving with their eleven-month-old son. "I told them to close the bedroom door at night so our two cats wouldn't go in," Jackie said.

Laura was certain she heard a cat in their room that night and woke Sam up, but when he looked, there was no cat. That same night, the diaper bag fell off the chair in their room three or four times, even though it was pushed as far back on the seat as it could go.

"Cat ghosts are a lot more common than human ghosts," Jackie said. "I saw one next to my dresser in that house when I was putting laundry away, lying on its tummy with all four legs tucked under it, looking up at me. I was startled, and then suddenly it wasn't there."

One day, Jackie was upstairs in the front office, just off the second floor balcony. "My left thigh started to burn, but it wasn't painful enough to do anything about, so I just kept working. When I took a shower, I saw that there were long, thin welts, like cat scratches, on my leg."

Gail noticed some rather unusual events herself. The bathroom that she used had an antique claw foot bathtub, deep enough for a really good bubble bath. On more than one occasion, after she turned off the taps from filling the tub, "The water was literally splashing around like an ocean. I said, 'Whoever's in there, just move over, because I'm getting in.' I never took anything like that real serious. I figured that if it didn't hurt me, I wouldn't hurt it."

Paul had a strange experience in that same bathtub. He was soaking in the water when he heard the doorknob jiggling as if someone were trying to open the door. Thinking it was his wife, he called out, "Jackie?" The rattling stopped.

"It wasn't me," Jackie said. "I would have just walked in because that door doesn't lock."

Another bathroom incident happened when Paul tossed some used q-tips into the toilet and flushed. Forgetting the plumbing had been modernized, Jackie stared in dismay at the swirling q-tips and said, "No, don't!"

Paul darted his hand in to pull them out, but they were gone. Jackie's first thought was that they had gone down with the water, but then she noticed the wet q-tips lying on the bathroom floor. She and Paul looked at each other, knowing that neither one of them had taken them out.

Barbie had a different take on the unseen bather. "I'd have my sister Shannon come in and read to me while I had a bath," Barbie said. "I was afraid I might drown while washing my hair."

The water-loving ghost wasn't the only paranormal thing that Gail came across in the mysterious old house. "I'd wake up at night and see someone standing at the foot of my bed in a suit with a wide-brimmed hat," Gail said. She was never particularly afraid of him. "My kids hated this attitude, but I decided that if something was going to happen, it must be my time to go." Gail wasn't afraid of the unexplained noises or the cold spots in the house, either.

Jackie has seen shadows in the same place that Gail spotted her visitor. A large shadow moved across the mirror over the mantle, completely blocking the reflective surface.

"Once our friend Jamin slept down here on a couch against the west wall," Jackie said. "He heard a clicking noise in the middle of the night, like bending window blinds, from around the corner of the next room. It sort of scared him. Every time he dozed off, it would start up, and every time he woke up it stopped. Jamin's not a believer in ghosts and he's not one to make things up. He doesn't care enough to make things up. He's an easygoing person, but he wouldn't sleep downstairs after that."

Then there was the unexplained flight of a curtain that had always stayed firmly in place by a couple of spring rods. Jackie was upstairs when she heard a commotion downstairs. She found a lace curtain that had covered a dining room window lying on the floor. It had to have flown fifteen feet across the room, clearing the table. One of the spring rods had caught in the doorway, stopping the curtain's flight around the corner into the parlor. Jackie could see no way that both spring rods could possibly have loosened enough to release the curtain, and couldn't explain why it would have flown across the room. "One of the ongoing stories about this house is that there's a lady that peeks out of the curtains," Jackie said. "When that curtain thing happened, it reminded me of that story."

The ghost was also on hand to entertain Gail Walker's

visitors. "My friend, Shirley, is like part of the family and would come and visit me. She'd go in the kitchen and get a drink and a sandwich, then set it down in the living room. Often if she left the room and came back, her food was moved somewhere she hadn't put it. She'd blame me." It was a natural assumption, since Gail and Shirley were the only ones in the house. But Gail hadn't touched a thing.

An antique clock that had once belonged to Gail's deceased friend, Mr. Softly, hadn't worked for years, but it looked good in the house since they were from the same era. One day, Barbie was astonished to see the clock's hands moving, yet no one had taken it in for repairs. "It had no working innards, but it worked in that house," Barbie said.

Not long after the Walkers moved in, Gail's sister, Carol, and her friend Janice came to visit from Arizona. Barbie stayed inside rather than going out to play with her sisters.

Gail was laughing at something Carol said when they heard furniture scraping above them.

"What are the kids doing upstairs?" Carol asked.

"That's not the kids," Gail said, as another chair-dragging sound filtered through the ceiling. "They're ghosts moving things around."

"Uh-uh!" Carol shot back, her eyes wide with disbelief.

"See for yourself," Gail said.

Carol looked out the front window and counted the kids lining up on the lawn for an impromptu game of Red Rover. They were all there.

Footsteps echoed above their heads.

"Someone's got to be up there," Carol insisted, standing up and heading for the stairs.

Gail and Barbie followed, with Janice trailing behind. When they reached the second floor, all was quiet and the rooms were empty.

The same thing happened to Jackie. She was in her bedroom on the second floor, talking to her mother on the phone, when she heard distinct footsteps overhead, accompanied by the squeak of the old wood floor. Keeping the phone to her ear, she walked up the spiral stairs to check it out, but the attic rooms were empty.

"It was like a friendly ghost," Gail said.

Yet it seemed to have something against Barbie's boyfriend, Shane. Barbie kept a picture of him in his National Guard uniform on her dresser. The first morning she woke up in her new bedroom, Shane's picture was moved to the very edge of the dresser top. Barbie asked everyone in the house who had moved the picture. No one confessed.

It was moved every morning, so Barbie simply scooted the picture back in place. "A few times I found it face down, but I'd just stand it up again," Barbie said.

On another bizarre note, in the two years that Barbie lived in that room, her light bulbs never burned out. But even more shocking is the fact that she never cleaned her room. "I never had to vacuum or dust that room because it was always clean," she said. Later on, she found out that the bedroom she used had once belonged to the doctor.

Jackie has lived in the house for nearly a year, and said that she has found the same thing to be true. She remembers vacuuming that room only once since they moved in, and she rarely dusts, as it always appears clean.

When Barbie lived there, the main bathroom had a small hole in the floor that opened into the basement. "I would rather run upstairs than use that bathroom, but if I had to use it, I'd cover the hole because I always felt like someone was watching me," she said.

Another strange feature of their new house is that it was always cold. "One time we went on vacation, and when we came back, the pipes had frozen and burst and there were icicles from the ceiling to the floor in the kitchen," Barbie said. "Once when I took my jeans out of the washing machine, they were frozen in the shape they had landed in the spin barrel."

Jackie agrees that the house always feels cool. Even

when the heat's turned up in the winter, she has to wear a sweater.

In a short, narrow hallway leading from the doctor's old waiting room were some drawers and a little door. "That's where my children played all the time," Gail said. "It was ironic because a couple of older ladies told me that's where they played when they were children and their parents brought them to see the doctor."

The Walker children spent so much time in there that eventually they noticed a wobble in the floor, which turned out to be a trap door. Once they pulled it up, they found a crawl space filled with a lot of wires, but there were also some things from the past, like a delicate old teacup and saucer, a glass syringe, a man's wedding band, a doily, and some antique medicine bottles. Barbie took the treasures and tucked them safely underneath everything else that nearly filled the cedar chest in her room.

"Before we took the things from under the trapdoor, the ghosts were doing things like practical jokes. After the "treasures" were moved, it was as if we had found a secret that had made someone unhappy," Barbie said.

Before and after Barbie's little sister, Sarah, was born, a baby could be heard crying in the house. "You'd sometimes hear a baby cry and you'd go check on Sarah and she'd be fast asleep," Gail said.

One night the door to Shannon's room slammed so hard that the old-fashioned ironing board stored upright in a narrow closet fell down to a horizontal position. "The next morning, there was the man's wedding ring that had been in the bottom of my cedar chest on the ironing board, along with a woman's wedding band that no one recognized," Barbie said.

"It looked like the woman's ring had been stepped on," Gail said. "It was smashed and old, with a diamond in it."

Things got worse after a relative came to visit.

"My stepson came with his wife and children from

Oklahoma. That's when I noticed a change," Gail said. "He was practicing with a ouija board, and I wasn't aware that he'd brought it in."

Gail told them to leave, but whatever unseen thing they brought in stayed.

"Paula had a desk like a cabinet, with shelves on it full of music boxes," Gail said. "The top half was thrown across the room. You could see claw marks on both sides of the cabinet." Paula was devastated when her treasured music boxes were broken.

Barbie grew to hate the darkness of night. There were at least three occasions when she was in bed, and her eyes suddenly flew open. She felt as if she were paralyzed. In a panic, she would command the presence to leave over and over in her mind until finally whatever it was would let her go and she would run downstairs.

About six weeks after Jackie and Paul moved in, Paul went to bed before Jackie and fell asleep facing the door. He woke up with the feeling that something stood behind him. He was frozen, not able to talk or move for a minute or two. He'd never been so scared in his life, but then the feeling went away.

One day Gail had to take Barbie to a dentist appointment in Provo. "I started to pull out of the driveway and something told me to stop."

"Mom started to cry," Barbie remembers. "I asked her what was wrong. She said that she had to take Sarah. I said, 'Okay, that's fine, go and get her.'"

"I went back in and got my three-month-old girl," Gail said. When they arrived home later that evening, the house appeared deserted.

"I thought my other children were hiding. I called, 'Where is everybody?' No one answered me," Gail said. With a rising sense of unease, Gail and Barbie searched the house, Gail calling for her children. At last she found them huddled together in an upstairs closet.

"Apparently they'd gone into the basement and went through some old medical bottles that were there. Smoke rose up and started toward them," Gail said.

The children backed up the stairs, yanked open the door, and ran as far away as they could get.

"After that, my children refused to live in that home. They said they weren't spending another night there, so we spent the night at our friends', Vic and Donna's, house." Gail called some men from her church and had a prayer.

"They said I needed a special blessing because I was the one the spirits were after," Barbie said.

"Right after the blessing, Donna and Vic took me back to the house to get some diapers and things," Gail said. "When I walked around the outside of the house, I could see the figure of a man with a pointed beard and black hair laughing at me from the turret window. That angered me."

Barbie said that she often saw someone up in the turret on the rooftop looking out.

"My friends saw it, too," Gail said. They told me, 'You do not go back in this home for anything.'"

In spite of the warning, Gail decided she needed to go back into the house once more. "My friends were at the cafe," Gail said. "I decided I was going to the house to get the diapers out of the dryer and get some clothing."

The laundry room was an add-on at the back of the house. "The door that went into the main part of the house was shut," Gail said. "As I reached for the doorknob that led to the dining room, something whispered, 'Don't go.' I felt the presence of something horrible."

Gail drew back from the door. "Trying to stay calm, I turned on some music while I waited for the clothes to dry. When they were done, I put them in the basket, then went into the kitchen. I heard this awful animal-type noise coming toward me. I picked up the basket, backed out the door, got in my car, and went to the café."

As soon as Vic and Donna caught sight of Gail's face, they were instantly concerned. "They asked what happened, because I was as white as a ghost. I said I couldn't describe what had been in that house."

When the family moved their things out, Barbie was surprised to find that all of the old treasures she'd tucked at the bottom of her cedar chest were gone, except the doily.

"In the basement is a tunnel that used to run under the street to an old house across the road," Gail said. "My brother-in-law, Joe, went down there and found a brick wall across the opening. He came back out because he said he couldn't breathe. We think the tunnel was used to help polygamists escape lawmen or maybe to hide from Indians."

Some people in town would cross the street rather than pass in front of the house.

Leon Olsen, a former owner, said, "Doris said that she would drive up and down the street and see an apparition in the upstairs window above the attic. As far as it goes, I actually had myself believing it, and my children also would justify that they saw this apparition in the window. I know that (my wife) Ruth and I would come home, and soon afterward the kids would report seeing the ghost. I've heard reports that some of those people seen were patients of the doctor."

Doris Larsen said, "Ruth was a no-nonsense person. She said to me, 'There are ghosts in this house.' There was no one else in there, and they could hear them walking around." Doris and her husband, MaCoy, would visit the Olsens from time to time. "It was the time of day it wasn't real light and it wasn't real dark, but there was something there," Doris remembers. "It was outlined like a person, but you couldn't see the features. It was framed in the front window on the second floor. We both saw it."

After Ruth Olsen died, Leon married Delila Nielson, who said that Leon always told her that the spirits in the house were friendly.

Barbie said that her mother likes adventure and is not one to be afraid. "She used to like old homes and re-doing them," Barbie said. "But now she likes to know the history of the house and what happened there before she'll buy it."

Once, after Barbie had moved out and established her own home with Shane, she thought seriously of going back to the house just to see what the new owners had done with it. That night she had a dream that she walked upstairs in the old house. She opened a bedroom door, only to see that two rooms had been combined into one lounge area with everything a person would ever need to live. Once she stepped inside, the door shut behind her and she knew she could never get out. She decided not to visit the old house.

The next owner, Claire Andersen, said that once she was in the former doctor's waiting room and heard a scrabbling, scratching sound, like mouse feet, moving around the room at about chest level. "A mouse couldn't move that fast through the framing in the walls," she said.

Claire also remarked that the man she'd bought the house from had undertaken major renovations on the place. He told her that he couldn't get any real work done until he'd cast the evil out several times.

"I've had a few eerie feelings," Paul said. "Downstairs by the fireplace I've had the hair stand up on the back of my neck, but it's gotten less since we've lived here. I feel perfectly fine now. I love the place, you know. I think most of the spirits or whatever lives here are good. It just feels like home, really."

"I'm 150% comfortable," Jackie said. "In California we had a house, but I never felt at home there. In this place, I felt completely at home as soon as we moved in."

It appears that the grand old house has finally left its troubled past behind.

The One Grave You Don't Want to Touch

It's a really bad idea to mess around with evil spirits.

Trey Chapman and his wife, Melinda, both worked in the cemetery business for so long that apparently some of the spirits began to believe the couple might be spirits, too.

"In the Evergreen Cemetery, there's a group of juniper trees where a playful spirit will peek out at you," Melinda said. "I never got a good look at it, because it peeks out when you aren't looking."

Melinda could sense it watching her, but whenever she turned to scan the trees for whoever was staring holes in her back, she'd just see movement. When she turned away, she'd see the ghost peeking from between the trees with her peripheral vision. "Maybe it's just shy," Melinda said.

In the city cemetery was a spook who wasn't afraid to get up-close and personal. "Whenever I went to a certain section, something would play with my hair," Melinda said. "My hair was short, and it felt like when someone takes a finger and flips the hair from underneath."

You'd think that if a ghost were so intent on giving you a new hairdo that it would touch you the fear would cause your hair to stand straight on end and spoil the new style. But not for Melinda. "It wasn't creepy; it was more annoying than anything."

Trey's responsibility as cemetery sexton was to locate

the proper place to dig a new grave. He'd done it hundreds of times and didn't think much of it, except that on one occasion, a grave was to be dug right next to a grave that had a reputation for being haunted. Trey was willing to admit that the feelings he got from that particular spot in the cemetery had him avoiding the place whenever possible, but he had a job to do.

"I should've waited until my crew was with me, but I didn't," Trey said.

Trey took hold of the metal probing rod that was used to determine the exact position of a grave's occupant, and pushed it into the ground. As expected, it touched the haunted vault. But then something totally unexpected happened.

"I've gone over the next few seconds in my mind a thousand times," Trey said. "But there's no denying that when that probing rod hit the haunted vault, a jolt of electricity shot through my body."

Stunned, Trey let go of the rod and stood staring at the ground. Shaking his head in puzzlement, Trey cautiously took hold of the probing rod again and worked it up and down, touching the vault again. "This time when I hit the vault, it felt like somebody shoved me viciously in the chest," Trey said. "I didn't hesitate. I took off running as fast as I could. My office was several hundred yards away, but I covered the distance in record time, praying all the way."

Covered in goose bumps and thoroughly terrified, Trey burst through the office door and slammed it behind him.

A startled teenage worker lifted his head. "Man, you look pale," he said. He moved over to Trey's side. "You okay?"

Trey nodded, too winded to speak. He decided not to talk about what had just happened.

"I've only told a handful of people about this," Trey said. "It was very real."

Because of his close working relationship with cemeteries, Trey knows that there are those who trespass into cemeteries and do things they shouldn't. "If they knew what they were messing with, they would run the other way," Trey said. "One girl I went to high school with experimented with bad stuff one weekend. It altered her whole personality, changing her from a bubbly, happy person to a basket case. If you take part in such things, in or out of a cemetery, you're a fool."

In spite of Trey's frightening encounter, the grave still had to be dug. This time, Trey had his crew with him when he probed for a location. "We didn't have any more problems," he said. Still, he placed the new grave as far away from the haunted one as he could, even though it would likely crowd the husband's future burial plot.

Where the invisible entity went is anyone's guess. "I figure I unleashed it, and maybe now it's gone for good," Trey said.

Boy with a Knife

Little children are often more perceptive than adults.

Matthew and Kristi had been in their rental home in Washington for only a month when they experienced an unsettling incident. The couple was getting their three-year-old daughter, Mallory, ready for bed. Mallory glanced into her room, wrinkled up her brow, and said, "I don't want to go to bed."

Kristi remarked, "It's late, and you need to go to sleep."

Mallory twisted her fingers around the fabric of her nightgown. "I'm scared of the man in the window, Momma. I don't want to go to bed."

After a moment of shocked silence, Kristi turned to Matthew, whose eyebrows were raised in surprise. "What does the man look like, honey?" Matthew asked.

"He has an owie on his face," Mallory said, tracing her finger down the side of her cheek. "And he's holding a knife." Her little fist clenched, mimicking holding onto something about the size of a knife handle.

Kristi felt a shiver run down her back.

"You must have had a bad dream," Matthew said.

"No," Mallory said, giving her small head a shake.

"Come on, I'll tell you a story," said Matthew, taking his daughter by the hand. "How about Cinderella?"

Mallory trailed reluctantly along behind her father. He

tucked her in between the covers and sat on the edge of her bed. Mallory gripped his trouser leg with her little fist and hung on. Three bedtime stories later, her grip finally relaxed and she fell asleep.

The next day, Kristi and Matthew had a talk with their landlady's son.

"Mom knows who lived there before you," he said. "I'll ask her."

That night, when Mallory hung back at her doorway, Matthew said, "Look, sweetheart, I chased the man away. He's gone."

Mallory glanced around her room with narrowed eyes before regarding her window with a solemn gaze.

"Daddy's the toughest Daddy ever," Kristi assured their daughter. "He can beat up anybody."

Matthew made a muscle pose with his arm, and Mallory stared up at him, considering. Then she allowed him to lead her to bed.

Before Matthew was through telling stories, the phone rang. Kristi answered it.

"Hello?"

"Hello, this is Virginia Wilson."

Kristi gripped the phone with both hands. It was their landlady. "Oh, hello."

"My son told me you had some questions about the people who lived there before you."

"Yes, we were wondering if there was a man who had anything to do with knives?"

"Oh, my, yes, a teenage boy who used to live there was absolutely fascinated with knives. He had quite a collection before he died."

Kristi felt a cold wave of apprehension wash over her heart.

Mrs. Wilson went on, "In fact, he was stabbed in a knife fight right there in the house."

"Stabbed in the face," Kristi said, certain that the owie

Mallory had described was the result of that incident.

"Oh, no, he was stabbed in the shoulder, but that's not what killed him. He was murdered a few months later on the other side of town. That's when his family moved out, you see."

Kristi felt as if a cold arm had slipped itself around her shoulders and pulled her in close. She tucked a trembling hand under one elbow and said, "So he wasn't stabbed in the face?"

"No, no. He did have a scar on his cheek, but that was from falling out of the tree in the backyard."

Kristi stared down the dark hallway that led to her daughter's room. "Well, thank you for calling," Kristi said, and hung up.

When Matthew came out of Mallory's room, Kristi told him what she'd learned.

It seems that discovering his identity took care of the problem, because after about a month of reassuring their daughter that Daddy had chased the man away, Mallory quit talking about him.

But Daddy kept telling her bedtime stories.

Shadows and Swords

Debbie Jean's mother didn't seem to realize that she had just saved her daughter.

In 1965, seven-year-old Debbie Jean had to share a double bed with her twelve-year-old sister, Maggie Dean. It was an arrangement that Maggie Dean would have rather done without, since she saw her little sister as nothing but a pest. But there were no spare rooms or even a separate bed available, so Mom said it had to be that way. Debbie Jean was sure that Maggie Dean would just as soon have her sleep on the floor, and she had no doubt that if she bothered her big sister, Maggie Dean would not hesitate to kick her out of bed. So Debbie Jean did her best to be as unobtrusive as possible.

One morning at about five, Debbie Jean woke up with a sudden, sick feeling in the pit of her stomach. Since Maggie Dean still breathed the slow and even breaths of one deep in sleep, Debbie Jean wasn't sure why she'd woken up or what made her feel so scared. She blinked her eyes in momentary confusion but held still for fear of jarring Maggie Dean.

Moving only her eyes, Debbie Jean peeked out the open bedroom door into the hall. What she saw just about stopped her heart. Two large figures carrying huge swords walked toward her open doorway. In the early morning pre-light, they appeared as dark shadows, one bigger than the other, the two of them broad enough to fill the hallway from wall to wall. Although Debbie Jean couldn't make out their facial features, she had the distinct impression that they were looking right at her.

"I thought they were after me," she said. "I was scared to death. I held onto my sister's pajamas, I was so scared, but I didn't dare wake her."

Debbie Jean watched the menacing shapes approach, step by step. Her heart fought so hard for escape, she was sure she was having a heart attack. If she cried out, she might wake her sister. If she cried out, they would know she'd seen them, and would run forward to drive their dark swords into her trembling body.

They had all but reached the doorway when Debbie Jean heard a door open down the hall. Her mother stepped out and strode toward the kitchen to help her husband get ready for work.

"Mom walked into the hall and went through the ghost guys like they weren't even there," Debbie Jean said. "I don't think she even saw them. They broke up and disappeared."

In case anyone doubts that what Debbie Jean saw was real, she says, "I know I wasn't asleep. I made sure I wasn't. I know what I saw."

Crackle Ghost

What made the eerie sound in the night?

"It was eight years ago, in 1998, when I stayed overnight at my sister's house," Bonnie said.

Bonnie had heard all the stories of when her sister, Erin, first bought the house and found awful graffiti scribbled on the upstairs walls. But Erin had done a good job of cleaning the place up, and the house's sordid past seemed to have stayed in its past. "I never paid attention to that kind of thing, nor did I particularly believe in it, or in ghosts," Bonnie said.

Delighted to be able to spend time with one another, the sisters stayed up late, talking and watching movies. "I don't remember what they were," Bonnie said, "But they were nothing scary. I don't like scary movies."

By the time they called it a night and went to their separate bedrooms, Bonnie was exhausted. "I went in and laid down and went right to sleep," she said.

Bonnie recalls that at about two o'clock AM, "I woke up suddenly with eeriness all around me. A strange sound filled the room, like the crackle of wind blowing through a plastic bag. But none of the windows were open." As the impossible sound grated against Bonnie's nerves, her skin prickled in fear.

"I felt this really eerie feeling," she said. "It was the

most eerie feeling ever. It was like somebody woke me up. I jumped out of bed and ran downstairs."

Not wanting to bother Erin, Bonnie curled up on the couch with an afghan wrapped around her. But it wasn't enough. "I was still shaking when my sister got up several hours later," Bonnie said.

Erin was more interested in than frightened about Bonnie's experience. She made her tell it several times, and even went upstairs to check out the room. Bonnie refused to go with her.

Although Bonnie still visits her sister, she has her limits. "I don't go upstairs in Erin's house anymore," Bonnie said. "And I definitely never sleep up there."

Covering the Mirrors

Why does the ghostly activity diminish when the mirrors are covered up?

Amie remembers the first of the strange events. It happened back when she and her sisters were young enough to need a babysitter.

"One night when Sydney was babysitting us, my sister Jeri was upstairs," Amie said. "She came running downstairs, screaming. Sydney went up to see what had scared her and got this bad feeling. Then she covered the mirrors in Jeri's bedroom."

Although that first incident happened several years ago, recent events keep the details fresh in the teenage girls' memories. There are still two antique mirrors in Jeri's old bedroom: a round one fastened on the back of a desk and a square one hanging on the wall. No one in the family knows if the mirrors are the cause for what haunt the room, but something certainly is.

When Jeri turned eighteen, she moved away to go to school. As the next oldest child, Amie decided to move into Jeri's room. She didn't have any competition, because by the time Jeri left, neither Brittany nor Manda, her younger sisters, wanted it. But Amie did. Part of Amie's desire to have her own room came from sharing a room with Brittany.

One night, Brittany started screaming. Her parents hurried to her room but couldn't wake her for awhile. They finally shook her, and according to Amie, "She woke up screaming so loud. She was kind of angry at them, but didn't remember screaming at all."

Amie might have been better off to stay roommates with Brittany, because after moving into Jeri's room, she became personally acquainted with the ghost.

"In January or February of 2004, at about two o'clock AM, something woke me up," Amie said. "Whatever it was threw something across my room. It rustled, pushing stuff around the floor. I don't know what it was, but it sure scared me. I ran down to my mom. She was already sitting up in bed, asking me what was wrong."

"My kids have had times when they've been scared out of their wits," Amie's mom, Enid, said. "One night, when we were all in bed, the children were restless. Then Amie came running downstairs, saying, 'there's something in my room.' If you're afraid, whatever it is feeds on your fear, making it stronger and giving it more power. I'm not afraid anymore. I go ghost hunting. I grab my flashlight and wander around the house, which always feels cold."

Sometimes, Enid gets clued in to ghostly activity from the ghosts themselves. "We've heard something walk up and down the stairs at night. I've heard what I thought was Amie walking around her room, but when I'd go up to check on her, Amie was fast asleep."

"After I moved out, I wouldn't sense the ghosts as often when I visit," Jeri said.

But they still make their presence known. "The other night when I was sleeping in Manda's room, someone sat on the bed and woke me up," Jeri said. "I don't know who was there. As silly as it may sound, since then when I've come back to visit, I have to have a hallway light on or something."

Even the family pets are in on the ghost visits. "We had an Australian Shepherd named Annie," Jeri said. "She got old and had health problems, so we had to put her down."

One night, Jeri sensed something watching her and woke up to see Annie standing at the foot of her bed, looking at her. Then she disappeared.

Peppy was a family cat that got so old he couldn't move, so they had him put to sleep. Enid has seen him a couple of times since then.

One night, the family was startled by the behavior of their little dog, Sammy. "Sammy was sitting on Dad's lap while we watched a movie," Jeri said. "Then she stood up and growled at the kitchen doorway. She started barking, and Dad tried to set her down on the floor, but she just jumped right back into his lap. She wouldn't get off, and she wouldn't stop. Something scared her. She finally calmed down after a couple of minutes."

The youngest sister, Manda, said that she once saw part of a ghost walking into the kitchen. "I saw the top half of a man walking past the table, but only half of his body," Manda said, sliding her hand down her own torso vertically, as if cutting herself in half.

"When I first moved into Jeri's room, I left the mirrors uncovered," Amie said. "But then I started covering them up, like Sydney did when Jeri was little, and since then, I've had no problems."

Enid, Brittany, Jeri, and Manda can see ghosts. Amie hears and feels them. But where they come from, and why they're there, no one knows.

"Mom checked the history of this house," Jeri said. "Nothing ever happened here. No one was killed. We're not sitting on a burial ground or anything."

Enid said, "Incidents with scary things have diminished since I've decided that when they come into my house, I'll say, 'Oh, you're here, let's find you and get rid of you. You're not welcome here.'"

Spirits of Hatred

One example of the tenacity of evil.

Loretta sat on the couch, facing Doug Christensen and the other two men she'd invited into her home to tell her about Jesus' teachings. Over the past few weeks, they'd visited half a dozen times, with Doug and his friends Jason and Andrew showing her scriptures, answering questions, and telling her more about Christ. While Loretta was always happy to see them, her husband, Mack, was not. If he happened to be home when they knocked at the door, he'd grab his can of beer and go in another room without a backward glance.

Although she usually wore a smile, on this visit Loretta seemed edgy. Leaning forward, she clasped her hands around her knees. Doug and his friends waited for her to speak. At last she asked, "Is there anything you can do to help get rid of the bad feelings in this house?"

The men looked at each other, then back at Loretta. Jason asked, "What kind of bad feelings?"

"Well, I really love my kids," Loretta said. "We like to go places together, and my two daughters are best friends. They're nice to their little brother, too. Whenever we're out of this house, I can feel the love between us so strongly, it's almost like a physical bond. But every time I get the family gathered together in one room of this house, it feels like we just want to kill each other." Loretta blinked rapidly, trying to keep her welling tears in check.

"Is someone going through a particularly hard time right now?" Andrew asked.

Loretta shrugged. "Well, it hasn't been easy for my kids to get used to Mack, even though we've been married for over a year. And weird stuff has been happening since we moved into this house six months ago." Loretta twisted her hands in her lap.

"What kind of weird stuff?" Doug prodded.

"Okay, you may think I'm crazy, but at night I'll lock my bedroom door and the master bathroom door. I know that sounds weird, but I'm kind of afraid of someone coming in the bathroom window at night. When they're both locked, then I can go to sleep. But on several mornings, I've found both doors standing wide open."

Doug said, "Your husband…"

"No, it's not him," Loretta interrupted. "He's already asleep and he sleeps like a rock. And it's not the kids, either. They don't have a key."

Loretta shifted forward in her seat and spread her hands as though beseeching her visitors for help. She lowered her voice and said, "My son goes downstairs and carries on conversations, but there's no one else down there." Doug felt a warning chill touch his heart.

He sensed that Loretta hadn't told them everything yet. After a moment of silence, he prompted, "Is there anything else?"

Loretta nodded. She hesitated, sighed, and then said, "You're going to think I'm crazy." No one answered. "A couple of times these past few weeks, when I wake up in the morning, I've found a spike driven into the wall."

Doug turned to see the startled faces of Andrew and Jason. He could only imagine that his own expression was equally surprised.

Jason spoke, "Is your son…" he stopped, unable to find

the words he wanted to say.

Loretta's mouth twisted in a mirthless smile. "If he or anyone else was pounding anything into the wall at night, I'm pretty sure I'd hear it," she said.

Jason ducked his head and nodded.

"I guess you're having a hard time believing me," Loretta said.

"I believe you," Andrew said.

At the same time, Doug said, "Well..." They both fell silent.

Loretta glanced from one to the other. Then she pushed herself to her feet and said, "I'll show you." She left the room, calling for her husband and children.

After a few moments, Mack sauntered into the room, his hands buried in his pockets. He leaned against the wall, pointedly ignoring the men.

Then came Loretta's children, two teenage girls and a gangly, pre-adolescent boy. They filed in, casting suspicious glances at Doug and the others. Finally, Loretta stepped into the room, and it suddenly felt as if the very air in the room grew darker. The girls turned on each other and began to argue, calling each other names until their brother punched one of them in the back. She whirled on him, her fingers extended like claws. Mack stepped in between and pushed them roughly apart, his hands curled into fists. Loretta screamed at him to leave them alone.

"It was one of the most powerful evil feelings I've ever felt," Doug said of the incident.

It was a relief when Loretta finally shooed her family out of the room.

After the voices of the family faded away, Jason said, "We could bless your house."

Loretta nodded her assent, a spark of hope in her eyes.

"Who would you like to do it?" Jason asked.

"Him," Loretta pointed to Andrew.

"Would you please bring your family back in?" Jason said.

Loretta stared at him in astonishment.

"They should all be here too," he said. "Don't worry, it will be all right."

Loretta left to gather in her family once again. Before long they were all assembled, their sullen faces hiding none of their resentment.

Andrew stood, bowed his head, and spoke the necessary words to engage God's most powerful assistance. Then he began blessing the house, piece by piece, starting with the shingles on the roof and working his way down. He mentioned the studs in the walls, the nails, plumbing, wiring, bathroom fixtures, even the doorknobs. He got to the ceiling of the room they were in, and then moved down the walls, including light switches and the furniture, and finally reached the floor.

"When he blessed the floor, Jason and I were sitting there on the couch, and could both feel something moving. I opened my eyes to see my pant legs wiggling like something was going down my legs," Doug said. "It seemed like the evil spirits were hanging onto my pant legs and didn't want to leave. I don't really know how to explain it. It's like kids running up and grabbing onto your calf, and when you step away, their hand slides off you."

After Andrew blessed the floor and the basement and the foundations of the house, he looked up to see everyone in the room smiling.

The darkness was gone.

The men assured the family that the evil could never come back in unless it was invited. Anything they did against the teachings of Jesus would bring it back, like watching bad movies, playing music with mean or suggestive lyrics, using violence against each other, even arguing or swearing. And the evil spirits would most certainly try to come back.

While Doug had this encounter with evil spirits, his sister discovered a haunted house several states away.

The lovely red brick house on a wide, pleasant street in a

rural western town had been the object of Leslie's admiration each time she drove past.

One day, she saw some men working inside the old house. She stopped to see if she could have a look around. She parked her car and walked to the open doorway.

"Hello?" she called. "Can I come in?"

One worker stood on a ladder, doing something with the top of a window so new it still had stickers on it. The other man sat idly on a windowsill. He hesitated at Leslie's question, but finally gave her the go-ahead with a nod. "Be careful of the glass," he warned, pointing at the floor.

When Leslie stepped inside, the dark interior of the house pressed in on her, a sharp contrast to the light from outside. She felt the crunch of shards of broken glass under her feet, and paused for a moment to let her eyes adjust to the reduced light. Soon, she noticed that in the middle of the floor was a big plywood patch that covered a dark opening into the basement.

"When I saw that hole in the floor," Leslie remembers, "I could feel that something bad had happened in that house."

Leslie skirted around the plywood patch and wandered through the dim, echoing rooms. "There was a washroom in the very back and I could feel evil very strong in there."

After Leslie had made a tour of the house, she went back to the construction workers. "Is it fun working here?" she asked.

"No," said the man on the windowsill.

"Why not?"

The man paused and looked up at the man on the ladder, who merely shrugged and went on working.

The man on the window ledge turned his eyes on Leslie. "We have to bring a witness just in case."

Leslie felt a chill run down her spine. "Just in case of what?"

"Because of them." He tipped his head toward the doorway. "If anything happens, or if something goes wrong, they need two witnesses to tell about it."

Leslie felt cold apprehension trickle down her neck. She was pretty sure the man wasn't talking about ordinary construction accidents. When Leslie glanced back at the doorway, she thought she saw a shadow.

With the uneasy feelings she got from being inside for such a short time, Leslie's no longer surprised that the house has been vacant for as long as she can remember. "Nobody will buy it," she predicted.

Cold Arms

An invisible party gave Dalene a most unwelcome embrace.

"Dalene!" her mother called up the stairs. "Rhonda's here!"

"Just a minute!" fifteen-year-old Dalene answered. She ran her fingers through her hair, slipped her bare feet into sandals, and gave her face one last check in the mirror before hurrying to the living room. Rhonda stood waiting, one knee cocked while she chewed a fingernail. When she caught sight of Dalene, she brightened and stretched her hand out to encourage Dalene to hurry.

Dalene's mother stopped them with a question. "When will you be home?"

"Um, probably by midnight," Rhonda said with a hopeful smile.

"How about probably by eleven o'clock?"

"But it's a weekend," Dalene protested.

"Eleven thirty. No later," Dalene's mother said with finality.

"Okay," Rhonda said, then turned and headed outside. Dalene followed, shutting the door behind them.

Rhonda whispered, "Mike and Tom and Cory are waiting for us."

Dalene glanced toward three dark figures huddled at the edge of the yellow beam cast by the streetlight in front of her house. One of them raised an arm to wave.

"What are we doing?" Dalene asked, hurrying after Rhonda as her friend jumped down the front steps and strode across the lawn.

"Karen's having a party," Rhonda said, "and we're going."

Dalene's heart raced. Karen was outgoing and reckless. A party at her house might be fun.

As soon as they reached the street, Dalene saw Cory's battered Ford Pinto pull up to the curb. They all climbed inside and drove to Karen's house. Light traced the edges of the curtained windows on either side of the front door while bits of rock music drifted in through the open car windows. There were no empty parking spots in front, so they pulled up to the curb nearly a block away.

Once they got inside, Dalene discovered that besides the friends she'd come with, there were very few faces she recognized. She noticed Karen standing in a corner, facing a small gathering, talking a mile a minute and laughing her head off. Karen was so busy entertaining that she didn't notice the newcomers.

"Hey," Tom said. "Check out the refreshments!"

"What about them?" Rhonda asked.

Tom grinned. "They've got booze!"

Dalene and Rhonda followed the guys to a table set up along one wall of the living room. The boys each grabbed a beer, but Dalene chose a can of Pepsi. She popped the top and took a sip. It was warm but comfortingly familiar. She hung onto it as she followed Rhonda across the room and the guys went their separate ways.

Before long, Rhonda struck up a conversation with a guy who scrutinized the girls with heavy-lidded eyes. Dalene didn't like the looks of him. For one thing, he was stingy with his smiles. After a few minutes of conversation, it was clear that Rhonda didn't share Dalene's feelings.

Dalene looked around the room, idly sipping her Pepsi. She wandered off to study some pictures on the wall more closely. One was a family group shot, with a little girl who looked like she could have been Karen. The Karen in the picture was about five years younger, and her smile looked genuine. The older Karen across the room forced another loud laugh. Dalene turned and saw that Karen's eyes were so camouflaged with dark liner that there wasn't much resemblance to the cheerful gaze of the girl in the photograph.

Dalene finished her Pepsi and set the can on a nearby table. She moved a few steps down a nearby hallway to examine an old wedding portrait on the wall.

Suddenly, a chill ran up Dalene's back, as though a cold draft had blown in, yet no one had opened the door. There wasn't any logical place that the cold air could have come from, but this was no passing breeze. Dalene was freezing, and with horrified certainty, she suddenly knew she wasn't alone. Something stood behind her, and whatever it was wasn't a bit shy. "It was like a pair of cold arms wrapped around me in a bear hug, but really tight," Dalene said.

Shocked by the unexpected grip and terrified of what she might see, Dalene looked down. Although her arms were drawn tightly into her chest, there was no one holding onto her. At least, no one she could see. But she could still feel the cold limbs wrapped around her, pinning her arms so tightly that she couldn't move.

"This was something I had never, ever, experienced before," Dalene said. "It was horrible. Oh, you just can't imagine. It was the most awful feeling."

Dalene stood in silent terror, shaking with fear. Goosebumps covered her skin, and her legs shook so hard, it was a wonder they even held her up.

In the next moment, she felt the grip loosen. As soon as she realized she could move, Dalene escaped the hall and went in search of Rhonda. She found her with the same guy she'd left her with.

Dalene interrupted. "I've got to go."

Rhonda turned toward her. "What's wrong?"

Dalene folded her arms across her chest and grabbed her elbows, trying to keep from shaking, but a sudden fear of the thing pinning her arms again made her lower her hands and clasp them in front of her. "Something grabbed me."

"Who?"

"I don't know, I couldn't see anyone, I mean, something was there holding on to me, but I couldn't see it."

Rhonda narrowed her eyes. "Have you been drinking?"

"No! Listen, Rhonda, you've got to believe me. It's hard to explain, but there was some kind of... I don't know. Something grabbed me and wouldn't let me go."

Rhonda's eyebrows raised in disbelief. "If it wouldn't let go, then why are you standing here?"

"It finally let me go. Rhonda, it was awful; it was the worst thing that's ever happened to me."

"That's too weird," Rhonda said.

"I have to go," Dalene said. "I can't stay here."

"You'll have to ask Cory if he's ready to leave. After all, we came in his car." Then Rhonda turned back to the heavy-lidded man. He turned up one corner of his mouth in a travesty of a smile that made Dalene shudder.

With a sense of urgency fueled by an image of impending doom, Dalene went in search of the guys. Spotting Tom and Mike standing together by the refreshment table, she hurried their way. As soon as she reached them, the lights in the room dimmed. Dalene could see people talking, dancing, and eating, but it was like twilight. The darkness was palpable, pressing against her skin with foreboding. If she'd had a knife, Dalene felt like she could have cut it apart.

"What happened to the lights?" she asked, a wave of apprehension crawling up her back, as if the unseen thing had followed her out of the hallway and now spread itself over the room, searching for her.

Mike glanced up at the ceiling, then back at Dalene. "Nothing. They're still on." He gestured upward with his beer can.

"No, it's dark in here," Dalene insisted. Even as she spoke, she felt the presence growing nearer. She couldn't bear the thought of those cold arms wrapped around her—she'd die if it happened again. Dalene took a step back, her frantic eyes searching the dim room.

"The lights are just the same as when we got here," Tom said. He wrinkled his forehead and searched Dalene's face. "What's wrong with you?"

"I have to get out of here," Dalene said, her conviction growing stronger with each passing moment.

"Why?" Tom asked.

Dalene took another step back. "I just have to go," she said, sure of her words. If she didn't leave now, the thing would get her. She felt eyes on her, drawing closer, then cold breath blew across her neck. "I'll wait for you guys outside," she gasped.

Dalene turned and ran for the door. She burst through and slammed it behind her, taking off at a run down the walk. Her apprehension eased as she moved further away from the house. She hurried to the battered Pinto to wait for her friends. They didn't seem in any hurry to join her, but she would wait as long as she had to. She would never go back inside that house, not for anything.

Eventually, her friends came out and drove her home.

"I never found out what it was," Dalene said. "But I hope I never get the chance to find out." She shuddered. "I never want to feel those cold arms again."

Evil Eyes

Fear can act like a magnet.

Although it's been thirty-six years since she heard the story, it still scares Stella Stevens just to think about it.

"When I was sixteen, I heard a story about the devil," Stella said. "These two guys were in their apartment and one of them said 'If I ever saw the devil, I'd punch him in the nose.'

"When they opened the door, a man stood there staring at them with mean eyes from under the narrow brim of his round derby hat. He said, 'Here I am. Punch me in the nose.'

"The guy who'd made the threat jumped back and his friend slammed the door shut. The first guy walked into the bathroom as though in a trance and picked up a razor blade. His friend followed him and stopped him before he could cut himself. He called a church leader to give the guy a blessing to cast Satan out. The whole story created a very vivid image in my mind."

Stella shivered. "I have a vivid imagination, and I could just see this guy in the derby hat, and I could see his eyes in my mind. A couple of nights later, I got ready for bed with my curtains closed, but when I turned off the light, I opened up my shades and got in bed.

"I was lying on my side. When I rolled over to get

comfortable, I could see there was a pickup truck sitting in the front of my house. You know how you open a vehicle door and the dome light turns on? That's what happened. This same man that I had imagined when I heard the story opened the truck door and the light came on. He was just sitting right there in the light, and I could see his face. He had that derby hat on, and his eyes pierced me. He was sitting there looking at me. I couldn't move or do anything. When I blinked, it all went away.

"I told my mother about it, but she didn't act like she believed me. For years, I didn't think anyone believed me, until one day I was babysitting my brother's kids, and my nephew said, 'Aunt Stella, did you see the devil?'

"It felt like a shock went through me. I couldn't think of what to say.

"'Grandma said you did,' he said.

"All those fears came rushing back, and I had to get a blessing. To this day when I close my eyes I can still see it. I'll never forget those eyes."

Possessed Mansion

These spirits don't want others to invade their territory.

"My mom was considering buying a home in Arizona and asked me to come and look at it," said Gwen Underwood. "It was a pretty big home, about ten thousand square feet. My friend, Meg, and I walked in the house and I got this creepy feeling right off the bat. As I walked around through the house, the creepy feeling followed me."

It took a while for Gwen to get all the way through the house. "Going down the back stairs, on the first floor off to the left, there's a chapel room. It's probably ten or twelve feet wide by twenty feet deep. You can look down this narrow room and at the end there's a stained glass window of what's supposed to be Jesus Christ, but it's an eerie looking thing.

"Then, as you walk into the room, there's this little door that leads into a three-by-four-foot room that's called the confessional. There's a little window in it. That room gave me the creeps."

The chapel wasn't the only place where Gwen felt uneasy. "There's a secret passageway where you can go behind the bookcase and open a door, and then there's a ladder going up inside to the closet of a second floor bedroom."

Gwen and Meg decided that it must be some kind of escape way. "Off that bedroom, you could exit onto a balcony and there were stairs out there."

Gwen described the closet as a "suitcase closet," with sloping ceilings. "It felt dark. It's not completely clear what went on there, but I had impressions of men with guns, drugs, and murder. Something went on in that house; I just don't know what."

Gwen and Meg tried to convince Gwen's mother that the house wasn't a good investment. Explaining their feelings and impressions didn't make any difference.

"My mother went ahead and bought the house," Gwen said.

"When she first moved in, there were lots of situations where light switches would turn on for no reason, and lots of things would break for no reason. The dishwasher would start without the button being pushed. Trees would blow down while they were landscaping and one knocked a fence over. They'd go to put in sprinklers and find they were broken. There were rats between the floor and the ceiling chewing on the wiring. I said to my mom, 'Something's going on in this house.' She had a couple of situations where she said that there was something there, and I said, 'I know, I've been trying to tell you!"

"The house was only ten or twelve years old," said Meg, "But I got feelings of really bad spirits there. We warned Gwen's mother not to buy it, and we told her why. She bought it anyway because it was a great price and it had acreage."

One of their mutual friends, whom they both described as very perceptive, told them that the house was on an Indian burial ground. She said that the Indians wouldn't be happy until the house was gone and their land restored. "The really mad spirits were Indians," Meg said. "This is why we think everything kept going wrong: appliances breaking, keys missing, pictures askew, and people getting sick."

Gwen's mother met an unsavory man when Gwen was about eight years old. She became curious and started reading up on things better left alone, her fascination drawing her to turn pages into the dark hours of the morning.

Suddenly, Gwen's six-year-old brother woke up and stumbled into his mother's room, sobbing about a nightmare he'd had. When his mother heard his bad dream, she realized that he'd dreamt about the very things she was reading about. Feeling it was a bad omen, she shut the book and never opened it again.

"She's pretty in tune," Gwen said of her mother, "But she didn't want to believe that anything was wrong with the big house she bought."

Gwen went on to say that her mother has prayed over the house, and since then, it's felt clearer. "It's much better than it used to be, but I haven't tried to stay the night there."

Gwen's affinity to feel spirits became apparent in her high school years. "I was fifteen or sixteen," Gwen said, "doing a research paper in high school on psychic powers. I believed in God and evil, but I hadn't really known about those forces and how they can enter your domain. I remember opening these books to do research, and my room just filled up with darkness. I picked up all those books and set them outside the house because I didn't want them in there. Then I picked up my scriptures and read them to clear it.

"I've learned that you can cast out darkness in the name of Jesus Christ," Gwen said. "If you've got the creeps, then negative energy is around and you can get rid of it."

Dark Portal

Listen to your feelings.

"I was dating my soon-to-be husband, and we'd gone to another scary movie," Diane said. "When I got home, I went to my bedroom upstairs. I used the snooze button on my alarm clock to listen to music before I fell asleep.

"There was no door on my room, but I'd hung some curtains for privacy. I was lying there listening to music, relaxing, when I heard someone say, 'Diane, get up and go downstairs.'

"I thought my mind was playing tricks from the scary movie I'd just seen, so I ignored the voice and snuggled into my covers. Again I heard, 'Diane, go downstairs.'

"This time I sat up, because it said it as plain as day. I thought to myself, 'Diane, you're really letting your mind wander. You've got to go to school in the morning, now just go to sleep.'

"I laid back down and I was just getting relaxed when the voice shouted, 'Diane! Now!'

"I opened my eyes in time to see my curtains pull apart and a dark figure with two glowing red eyes walk through. I was shaking, sweating, and freezing, all at the same time, more scared than I've ever been in my whole life. I grabbed my blanket and pillow, dodged around the thing, and fell down the narrow, steep stairs of our old house. I ran into my parent's room, shaking so badly that I couldn't talk.

"Dad looked at me and knew what had happened. He got some friends to help him get rid of it. Something has followed me since then, and if I'm not careful how I live my life, it comes back."

Diane had been married for about ten years and was home alone with her children. Learning her lesson from her teenage years, Diane says, "I was being a good girl. I watched *The Little Mermaid* with my children before they went to bed, then I went to my room.

"I was restless. *Something's not right*, I thought. The dog was barking. I was scared, but I thought I was letting my imagination run away with me.

"I rolled over in bed, but then my eyes suddenly popped open wide, and I thought, *Oh my gosh, something's in the house*."

Diane didn't see anything, but she could feel it. "I keep nightlights on, so I could see my door opening, but I couldn't see anyone there. Something rushed across my room and crawled over me. It's not a fun feeling to be mauled by an evil spirit. Every hair on your body stands out. It didn't hurt, but the fear and panic is unbelievable. I felt cold, not wet like snow, but a creepy, eerie feeling."

It was hard for Diane to move in order to cast the evil spirit away from her, but when she finally did in the name of Jesus Christ, it backed off.

Diane's husband wasn't home, and her father was dead, so she was on her own. With shaking hands she put a scripture video into the VCR, then hunched herself in front of the television set, not daring to get more than five feet away from the screen. She watched the movie over and over until she was so exhausted, she couldn't stay awake.

"I went into my room and grabbed my scriptures and laid them open on top of my chest."

Since she watched horror movies as a teenager, Diane says, "I feel like there's been something after me all my life. Now I'm very careful what I allow in my home. We completely avoid horror and violent movies.

"I'm a true believer that movies have an aura about them. Ultimately, if it's a feel-good movie, the good enters your home. I think that horror movies are like opening a portal for the evil to come through.

"Maybe that thing in my bedroom when I was a teenager wanted to possess me. If it could possess me, then maybe it would have had me commit suicide; I don't know.

"I've learned a few things. When you use the name of the Lord and Savior, it's sacred and serious and has a lot of clout with it. I didn't like being afraid, so I'm not afraid anymore. I couldn't adequately protect my children if I was that scared. If it can't scare you, it has no power and it leaves."

Imaginary Friends

The apartment came with a friendly boy and a vicious one; both were invisible.

In September 1988, when she was five months pregnant, Anna moved with her husband, John, and nearly three-year-old daughter, Jessica, into an apartment. While Anna was still working at unpacking boxes, Jessica made a startling announcement. "She said there were two boys," Anna said. "One was called something like Zachariah, and one was called Babel."

When Anna questioned her daughter about them, Jessica described her invisible playmates: "Little, like me." She said that Babel was older, but she didn't like him, because he was mean. She said that Zachariah didn't like Babel either.

Anna thought it was kind of cute that when Jessica was in the tub, she pretended that Zachariah was in there with her. She'd splash and laugh and carry on toddler conversations with him.

"My next-door neighbor's little boy, Devin, used to come over and play, but then one day Capri called and said Devin didn't want to come over anymore. She said that someone my daughter played with was mean," Anna said. "At the time, Jessica hadn't played with anyone but Devin."

Anna liked things tidy, and keeping Jessica's toy box in her closet seemed an ideal solution, but Jessica refused to go in there. Eventually, her mother relented and pulled the toy box out of the closet.

One night, Anna was startled awake by the sound of Jessica's cries. Jessica said she was terribly afraid of Babel, insisting that he lived in her closet.

"So many times she cried out in the night and I made her go back to her room," Anna said. "I thought she was making it up. However, a month later, things started happening to me.

"As soon as it hit midnight, our touch-tone phone would start dialing, even though it was hung up. My answering machine would beep. Then I could hear somebody walking around the house, but since John worked the graveyard shift and wasn't home, I was always too scared to check it out," Anna said.

The closer it got to October 31st, the more frequently things happened. Starting two weeks before Halloween, Anna heard things every night, and if Jessica came wandering into her mother's room looking for comfort, Anna was more than happy to invite her daughter to crawl into bed beside her.

Oddly enough, when Halloween passed, the midnight noises became less frequent. It was a slight comfort, though, because now the police reported a flesh and blood rapist prowling the neighborhood.

John decided to help his wife protect herself. One day when Jessica was at her grandmother's, John took Anna shopping. "He bought me a pearl-handled pistol," Anna said. Then they picked their daughter up from Grandma's house and went home with no intention of letting Jessica know that Anna had a gun.

But it didn't matter.

"Jessica went into her room, and then came back out and told us that Babel said he was going to get the gun when Dad was gone to work."

Anna was shocked. John was stunned. Then they packed up their belongings and spent the night at Anna's parents'. "My dad thought I was insane," Anna said.

The night away was only a brief reprieve. Anna didn't want to go back, but they couldn't get out of their lease.

It seems that Anna's nocturnal visitor decided to check and make sure she had returned. Her bedroom window was covered with metal blinds, the kind that make a soft yet distinctive "clink" when someone parts them with their fingers to look out. Once, after midnight, Anna heard someone walking around her bed. "Then I heard the blinds clink. I looked over and they were open in just one spot, like someone was looking out." After awhile the blinds closed, but Anna couldn't sleep. She stayed awake, frozen with fear, until her husband got home at five o'clock in the morning.

Toward the end of January, Anna gave birth to a baby boy. She and John named him Zachary. It was only years later that Anna realized how close her son's name was to that of Jessica's invisible playmate. Then she wondered if their little boy could actually have been the spirit that Jessica enjoyed playing with as a toddler.

A couple of weeks after Zackary was born, the family moved out of the apartment.

Anna doesn't know why they had ghostly roommates, unless Zachariah was really her son, getting acquainted with his big sister before he was born. But where Babel came from is a mystery.

Part 3

Mischievous, Annoyed, or Benign Spirits

In the Path of Forever

They weren't trying to hurt anyone, only drive them away.

In 1981, Sondra Russell found herself immersed in a whole new culture when she moved with her husband, Jack, to Lame Deer, Montana. His new job had taken them to the northern end of a Cheyenne Indian Reservation.

They settled on a plot of land halfway up a gentle slope. It didn't bother Russell a bit that an Indian cemetery, set slightly farther up the incline, overlooked their new place. It seemed that it would be a quiet, peaceful spot to live, since it was a little removed from another trailer house below them and few other houses scattered further out on the flat.

The land was leveled, a trailer was brought in, utilities hooked up, and the Russells moved in. It took a few days to get things put away, especially working around their four young children, but Sondra managed while Jack was busy with his new job at the sawmill.

Sondra didn't notice anything strange until a few days after she set up housekeeping. "Our bedroom was at the very back, closest to the cemetery," Sondra said. "I was in bed and I could feel something heavy leaning on me, pushing down on me. I opened my eyes and looked, but I couldn't see anything. Then, when I turned the light on, it went away."

Sondra told Jack what had happened, but he just thought she was overreacting to a bad dream. Even when it happened again, he didn't think anything of it.

"My husband never felt it or saw it until the night I called out," Sondra said. "This time I saw lights flashing on the ceiling. They were moving back and forth."

When Sondra yelled, her husband jolted awake in time to see the white flashes. A light colored cloud flew from the room with a "whoosh" of sound, drawing air behind it with enough force to slam their bedroom door shut.

"What was that?" Jack asked, sitting up in bed, his eyes wide.

"It's what I told you," Sondra said. "Something's been here in the night."

The next few nights were calm, but then strange things started happening in the daylight. After her older children left for school, Sondra heard water splashing in the bathroom sink. When she went to investigate, she found the faucet running. She turned it off, and decided to have a talk with her children when they got home from school about not being so careless.

A short time later, she heard splashing again. When she went to check, she found the faucet turned on yet again. She knew she hadn't done it, and she knew that her one-year-old daughter, Jessie, couldn't have done it, either. Jessie wasn't even tall enough to see over the top of the counter. They were the only two people home.

Jack had a hard time believing Sondra when she told him about the faucet that turned itself on, but he couldn't doubt the tapping noise that soon began sounding from the closet.

The children noticed it first, since it came from the closet in their room. A nearly constant "tap, tap, tap" sounded through the closet door.

Since the trailer wasn't yet skirted, Sondra and Jack went outside to investigate. But even though Jack crawled underneath to check, he couldn't find any reason for the noise.

The tapping continued.

The water kept turning itself on.

Doors slammed themselves shut.

Sondra did her best to ignore the strange events as she took care of her family and settled into their new community.

One day, Sondra and her children went on a day's logging run with Jack and some other workers in a section of the mountains around Lame Deer. Sondra took the children for a walk in the woods while the men worked. Holding little Jessie's hand, she lagged behind her older children.

Suddenly, her children came rushing back to her, a brown bundle in their arms, crying, "Mom, Mom, we found an old, old doll!"

Curious, Sondra took the doll to examine it more closely. It was wrapped tightly in strips of ancient leather. The face was brown with age, the eyes shut as if asleep. It looked as if the doll was made of leather, too, but it only took a few moments to arrive at the horrifying realization that what she held was no doll, but a mummified Indian baby.

"Where did you get this?" she demanded.

"We'll show you."

Her children led the way to an area behind a low hill. A number of round holes, like little caves, came into view. When Sondra got close enough, she bent to look inside one of them. She made out several shadowy figures, some adult-sized, but more of them smaller ones.

A chill wind blew across her neck. Sondra straightened and scanned the strange place with her eyes. Her heart nearly leapt out of her chest when she saw a wizened figure sitting at the edge of the eerie place. Out in the open was one lone Indian sentinel, an aged woman using a rock as a backrest. "It looked as though she'd been sitting there for so long that she'd actually been petrified into the rock itself," Sondra said, but she didn't dare tug on the corpse's primitive leather dress to find out.

When one of Jack's Cheyenne coworkers heard about the children's discovery, he took the baby from Sondra and returned it to its resting place. Then he faced the Russells. "You must never come back here again."

"The children didn't mean anything..." Sondra began.

"I know," the Indian interrupted.

"What happened here?" Jack asked.

The Indian fastened his deep black eyes on Jack. "Smallpox. Many, many years ago, before the time of my grandfathers."

Then he swept the children with a stern gaze. "You must never, ever come back here. You must never think to take anything, not a leather pouch or pipe, not even a single bead."

The Russell children nodded their heads solemnly.

The Indian's eyes shifted to Sondra. "Never touch anything again." He looked back at the children. "It's a good thing you are innocent children. If that had been an adult who had taken the baby and gone away with it, it would be really bad for him."

"How bad?" Jack asked.

The Indian was silent for a moment before he said, "There was this guy, name of Sunny Black, who used to work here. His wife liked to walk around the cemetery. She had this problem of wanting to pick up odds and ends of things left on the graves. Everyone told her not to touch them, but she didn't listen. She'd take them home and show Sunny, and he'd tell her 'you're not supposed to touch that stuff.' It didn't make any difference; she kept on doing it.

"She was only in her thirties, but she got this mysterious disease that made it so she couldn't talk or walk. She ended up in a wheelchair for the rest of her life."

"What was the disease?" Sondra asked.

"Nobody knew," the Indian said. "It was a strange disease, or curse. You see, because of it, she could never visit the cemetery again, except to stay. She died."

The Indian turned back to face the village of the dead and began singing a strange, eerie singsong chant, a prayer to rededicate the site as the resting place for the people who died there.

Sondra took her family home, but she couldn't seem to get the strange Indian cemetery out of her mind.

One day, she couldn't stand it any longer and took a friend with her to show her where it was.

"I had no intention of going near it," Sondra said. She just wanted to point it out to her friend, and maybe let her catch a glimpse of the old woman melded with the rock. But even though she went to the same place and followed the same trail that she had on the day she'd gone walking with her children, she couldn't find the ancient site again. "I guess when they say don't mess with something, they mean it," she said.

The Native Americans on the reservation received regular commodities such as cheese, eggs, and crackers from the government. Sometimes they would sell their commodities, and sometimes the Russells would buy them.

The strange thing about the transactions is that the Native Americans would drive to the end of the Russells sloping driveway and honk their horn. When Sondra looked outside to see who was there, they would shout, "Do you want to buy commodities?" She couldn't figure out why they didn't just drive up to the house.

One day she asked the man she'd just bought from, "Would you help me carry this? I don't think I can pack it all."

"Oh, no," the Cheyenne said, eyeing her house with suspicion. "I won't go up there. There are too many weird spirits floating up around your house."

Sondra had to carry it herself.

"These people can be very spiritual," Sondra said. "They believe in certain things and you don't ever cross anything they believe. If they feel they sense something, they won't go there. All of them felt something funny where we lived, and they'd never go up on the hill."

It was about six months after the Russells moved to Lame Deer when Sondra got up one morning to find all three of her older children piled on the front room floor, criss-crossed over each other like sticks laid out to build a campfire. She stared at them for one shocked moment before she asked, "What are you guys doing out here?"

Her children stirred, then opened their eyes and blinked up at her. They glanced around in confusion as they slowly untangled themselves.

"I don't know," eleven-year-old Terry said, pushing himself up onto his knees and looking around in bewilderment.

"Mommy, Mommy," cried Tanya, standing up and stumbling over to her mother, her six-year-old face twisted with confusion.

"Where are we?" asked eight-year-old Mandy, rubbing her bleary eyes. "What are we doing sleeping in the living room?"

None of her children had any recollection of leaving their bedrooms the night before.

Jack was so shaken by the bizarre event that he mentioned it to his coworkers.

"Has anything else happened?" one of the Cheyenne asked. Jack told him about the other strange events.

"How long has it been going on?"

"Almost since the day we moved in," Jack said.

"Your house needs to be cleansed," the Indian told Jack. "You've got to get the spirits out."

"How do I do that?"

The Indian surveyed Jack with an intense gaze, his eyes so black they looked like wells sunk deep into ancient tradition as he waged some internal battle. At last he gave Jack a single nod of his head and straightened his back, as though the battle had been won.

"I know a purification ritual. I will come over after work."

He was the first Indian to enter their house. As soon as he stepped inside the doorway, he stood still, as if listening. Then he walked through the rooms, his tread soft and careful as though afraid of waking the spirits. He ended up in the kitchen.

"These spirits aren't out to hurt you," he said. "They just want you to move."

Surprised, Sondra asked, "Why?"

"You're in their path."

Jack glanced at Sondra, then turned back and asked, "What path?"

"It's part of the circle of their world. Your house is set too far back. You're in the path they use to go from this life into the next and back again. It disturbs their peace. I don't know if I can do this alone, but I'll do my best."

The Indian took a piece of sagebrush, wrapped it with twine, and lit it on fire. Then he walked throughout the house, chanting something in the Cheyenne tongue.

After that, the tapping, running water, and slamming doors lessened somewhat, but they were still there. He came back three more times to conduct the same ritual. After each visit, the mischief lessened.

Finally, the Russells made arrangements to pull their trailer house about a foot farther down the slope from the cemetery. As soon as they did, the strange occurrences stopped.

The Russells lived for another five and a half peaceful years in that trailer on the cemetery hillside, next door neighbors to the portal that the Indian spirits used to cross from this world to the next and back again.

"It was so strange. They did the weirdest things, but they were never mean to us," Sondra said. "Still, it was enough that it really scared you."

Waking the Dead

Why would ghosts haunt a brand new house?

Stephen and Lara Carson jolted awake at the sound of their thirteen-year-old son, Kyle, screaming.

"I dashed out of my bed and down the stairs, followed by my wife," Stephen said. "Kyle said he'd heard some strange noises. He was convinced that something was just outside of his door, in the basement. It was four o'clock AM."

Later, Kyle said that he'd been startled by his watch alarm going off. Yet there was definitely something strange brewing in the unseen spiritual fiber of the Carson's house.

"Not more than a couple of weeks later, I had my encounter," Stephen said. "I woke up on this particular night with the impression that one of my children had entered the room." It wasn't uncommon for the Carson's four-year-old daughter to wander into their bedroom at night and climb in bed with them. Occasionally, the older children would go looking for their parents in the night too, if they weren't feeling well, or had a bad dream, or heard the creaks of a new house settling in the quiet dark of night.

"I turned over in bed expecting to see my youngest child preparing to slip into bed with us," Stephen said. "Imagine my surprise when instead of seeing my daughter, I saw a glowing figure at the foot of our bed. I was still somewhat asleep and so it took a moment for me to realize that this was not a real person but some kind of ghostly apparition.

"Though the idea of ghosts being real is not too far-fetched for me to believe, the idea of having my very own experience of encountering one was a bit overwhelming. Like a frightened child, I pulled the covers over my head and quickly wished the unwanted visitor away. With a strong heart-felt prayer, I asked for the visitor to disappear, to leave and not return.

"Finally gaining enough strength and courage to pull the covers back, I cautiously peered from the side of my eyes to see of such a being was still in my room. To my relief, it was not."

Stephen was puzzled by the appearance of a ghost in his brand new house. They'd only moved in two months earlier, so there was no possibility that any previous occupants had met an untimely death within those walls. Stephen couldn't quite figure it out. Although hatless, the ghost had the appearance of an old cowboy. "Definitely from a hundred years ago, like the turn of the twentieth century," he said. "I have to wonder if there's any unmarked grave of an old settler who died here. I felt that spirit was kind of looking in just trying to figure out what was going on."

Lara slept through the whole thing.

As for Stephen, "I have no explanations, but it took me a good hour to fall asleep again."

Later, Stephen heard a story from a woman in her 90s. When she was a girl, her father told her that in the late 1800s, two men had a fight over irrigation water in the very same area that Stephen's house now sits. One of the men became so angry that he struck the other man with his shovel and killed him on the spot.

Still Skating

More than one unusual thing goes on in this old warehouse.

In its glory days, it was a roller skating rink, a popular social spot filled with vibrant life and the sound of skating music mingled with metal wheels smacking polished wood in a rhythmic cadence. A chorus of voices from bass to soprano called back and forth, sprinkled with raucous laughter and cries of children who'd been surprised by wheeled shoes rolling right out from under them, tossing them onto an unyielding floor to bruise bottoms or knees.

Somewhere in its shadowed history, the building also served as an amateur boxing arena. There's an old man in his 80s who claims that in the 1950s, a boxer was killed during a fight there.

Maybe it's the dead boxer who's haunting the warehouse, looking for a sparring partner, or maybe it's a previous owner who committed suicide.

But did either one of them ever roller skate?

Now the old building serves as a warehouse, where more than one person has encountered a ghost.

Helen is one of them.

Helen's a mature, even-tempered former employee who was working on filling orders one day when she heard someone whistling. It wasn't the urgent kind of whistle that calls you to attention or signals for you to come closer, it was just an idle tune that filled the air. At first Helen thought someone was working on the other side of the shelves, but when she moved around the end of the stack to see who it might be, she found that she'd been mistaken. She was alone.

On another occasion, Helen was busy at work when a man spoke from behind her. "Helen."

Startled, she turned to see who had come up on her so quietly that she hadn't heard so much as a single footstep, but there was no one there. Puzzled, she walked around the shelves, searching for whomever it was that had called out to her. She saw no one. She heard nothing, not even the sound of retreating footsteps, quiet breathing, or muffled laughter. Goose prickles rose on Helen's arms in the eerie silence.

It seems that the ghost has other talents besides whistling and memorizing the employee's names.

Late one night, another employee named Audrey made a quick stop to the warehouse in order to return a computer to the office. When she let herself into the reception area at the front of the building, she was startled to hear a deep voice calling out what sounded like skating announcements. The voice came from behind the door at the far side of the office, which closed off the warehouse section.

More curious than afraid, Audrey set the computer down on a nearby desk, walked over to the door, and pushed it open. She couldn't see anyone moving about in the dim interior. Indeed, there was no room to roller skate unless the ghosts were moving between the narrow shelves that had been set up on what had once been the skating arena floor.

Yet Audrey could hear a male voice echoing in a hollow cadence as though speaking into a microphone in order to be heard over the rhythmic "swoosh, swoosh," sound of skates rolling across the polished hardwood flooring.

"Everyone find yourself a partner, it's couples' skate time. Find yourself a pretty partner or a strong arm to lean on, because there are no singles al..."

Abruptly the voice cut off, as though the ghostly announcer had suddenly caught sight of Audrey. A cold chill slipped up Audrey's arm and snaked across her shoulders, lifting the hair on the back of her neck and spewing cold shivers down her back.

Now much more afraid than curious, Audrey turned and fled the building.

Karl was another employee who had to make a late night merchandise drop at the old warehouse. It was a cool, dark evening when he pulled up to the building at around ten PM. He unlocked the front door before hoisting the heavy box in his arms and stepping inside. Not bothering with the lights, Karl moved to the nearest desk and dropped the box onto it.

In the sudden silence, he heard the floor behind him creak as though someone were moving across the old floorboards toward him with careful, measured steps. Karl's heart kicked into high gear and he spun around to see who it was. In the instant that he realized no one was there, the floor behind him let out a soft squeak as though someone were trying to sneak up behind him. He whipped his head around and anxiously surveyed the empty room.

Yet it was empty only to his eyes. "I could sense the spirits in there," he said. They seemed to be walking on all sides of him, the floor creaking at odd intervals, as if all the beings were jockeying for the best vantage point to examine their late night visitor.

Suddenly, the water cooler at the side of the room started to bubble furiously, like a miniature enclosed Jacuzzi. "It was going absolutely crazy," Karl said. "I'd never seen it do anything like that before, and I've never seen it since."

Karl's trembling hand darted out and flipped on the light. As though it were wired to the same switch, the water cooler instantly quit bubbling. Karl watched in morbid fascination as the turbid water swirled its way to a gradual stop.

"Things were definitely not normal that night," Karl said. "I got out of there."

Perhaps more than one ghost inhabits the warehouse, because at least one disembodied female voice was reported by Brett, another employee who had a late night warehouse adventure. He was working after hours in his office when the phone intercom beeped and the voice of his coworker, Candace, said, "Brett, come down to my office right now. I need to talk to you."

Brett pushed himself away from his desk and walked over to his office door. He opened it to find the building dark and eerily silent. He hadn't realized it was so late.

Uneasy, he hurried to Candace's office without encountering a single other person along the way. He couldn't hear anyone else moving around, either. A chill crept up his spine, and it was with a distinct sense of relief that he took hold of Candace's doorknob. He really didn't want to be alone.

Brett opened the door, fully expecting to see Candace sitting at her desk. Instead, he faced a dark room. Candace wasn't there. No one was.

"I hadn't realized that I was the last one in the building," Brett said. "It was eerie."

The next day, Brett discovered that Candace had gone home for the day an hour before his intercom had delivered a message in a voice that sounded uncannily like hers. No one else admitted to being there, and Brett believed them. If someone had been trying to play a prank, Brett would have heard or seen them leaving Candace's office.

Brett quit staying at work late or going in after hours. And as far as anyone knows, the ghosts are still there, playing with the intercoms, skating around the warehouse, and getting drinks from the water cooler in the dark of night.

A Single Candle

What caused the mysterious lights in the windows of the old house?

Ben Russell served on the police force in Maryland in the 1970s. One day, he and a fellow police officer made a decision. "Me and my friend heard so much about ghosts that we went searching for them," Ben said. "I was on the east coast, where the history goes way back to the 1600s. We decided that we were going to find a ghost."

The two officers were on the night shift, which made their ghost-hunting plan even easier. "We got a ouija board, and at midnight we played with it over the grave of William somebody—I don't remember the last name—who died in 1640," Ben said. "He was an original Maryland colonizer. We asked it questions like, 'Who will be the first to die?' and the answer was something stupid, like, '#3.' It just didn't make any sense, so we decided that it was a bust."

Ben and his partner visited various places that they'd heard were haunted. They went walking in haunted fields. They sat outside the house of Mary Surrat, the first woman hung in the United States. Although she professed innocence throughout her trial and all the way to the gallows, Mary had allowed those who were convicted of assassinating President Abraham Lincoln to hold meetings in her house, so she was found guilty of aiding and abetting.

"We went into the basement of that house, but nothing happened," Ben said. "We went through other houses, but none were haunted."

At least, not until Ben found himself on a night shift by himself.

He doesn't remember why his partner wasn't with him. All he knows is that at around two o'clock AM he saw something that's awfully hard to explain.

"I parked off the road in front of an old abandoned house that was built in the 1700s," Ben said. "A light appeared in one of the lower windows, and I thought somebody was in there. I was certain no one lived there, so I thought it was probably some teenage kids who were working to perpetuate the ghost myth. It was a contained spot of light that moved behind the windows as though someone walked with a candle in their hand. I watched it go horizontally across the bottom floor of the house, and then it disappeared for three or four seconds. When I saw it next, it was shining through an upper window." Yet there had been no time for a candle bearer to take a flight of stairs and reach the top.

"How do you explain that?" Ben asked. "It was really odd. It makes you wonder."

Some might say that there was more than one person in the house, but Ben only saw a single light.

"It was very unlikely that they were already in there, just waiting for someone to park off the road," Ben said. "And how would they get the light to go from one floor to the other in such a short time?"

Ben watched for at least fifteen minutes as the candle moved from window to window and floor to floor with never enough time in between for anyone to use a flight of stairs.

"It was weird," Ben said. "First it would go horizontal, then up, then horizontal, then down, then horizontal. It's the kind of thing you look at and figure there's got to be an explanation, but I don't know what it could be."

After that experience, what does Ben have to say about the supernatural?

"I don't believe in ghosts," he said.

Indian in the Kitchen

A visit from a curious ghost.

Teri Rodeman could be one of those people who have a natural affinity for seeing spirits, as evidenced by an experience she had as a young woman.

Many years ago, she had graduated from school but was still living with her parents in Huntington Beach, California. With her parents on vacation, Teri was staying alone.

"I got off work from the late shift and arrived home at about 11:30 at night. I didn't turn many lights on, but I didn't feel ready to go to bed. I was listening to the stereo and sitting on the loveseat in the living room. It was around midnight or a little after, and it was rather dark in most of the house.

"I looked into the kitchen where all the lights were off, and saw a dark shape standing by the refrigerator. I was startled, since I thought I was alone. The strangest thing is that the figure in the kitchen was an Indian man dressed in full Indian regalia. He just stood there, looking at me. I was scared, too scared to move, but after two or three minutes, he disappeared."

Once the spirit was gone, Teri said, "I felt curiosity from him, as though he was wondering what I was doing there."

Teri regained her composure long enough to get up off the loveseat and go to bed, taking a wide berth around the kitchen. Once she was calm, she wondered why there would be an Indian ghost in her house in Huntington Beach. When she thought back over the history of the area, she realized that there must have been Indians living there centuries before, or at least passing through.

Perhaps the Indian she saw in her kitchen was buried in the ground beneath the house. Maybe he'd been killed on that very spot, and felt an attachment to the place where his spirit had separated from his body.

Another possible explanation for Teri's ability to see the Indian apparition is the Indian ancestry she lays claim to.

"My great-grandfather was a Sioux and Choctaw. My cousin looks one hundred percent Indian, since he has the skin and hair color. My dad had brown eyes and a darker complexion, just like grandmother did," Teri said. "My great-great grandmother was a medicine woman from Mackinaw Island, Michigan. Her name was Mary Minor, but her Indian name was Whitesides."

As an interesting side note, Teri's great-grandfather did the artwork for the Indian head on the side of the Calamut Baking Powder can. Maybe the Indian she saw was him, checking the kitchen cupboards to see what brand of baking powder his descendents used.

Ghosts in the Bathroom

Three accounts of rather rude ghosts.

Mavis put her face under the shower spray, letting herself relax as the water riddled her tired body with tiny bullets of warm liquid heat, soothing her tense muscles until they felt as soft as clay.

With her young son, Tad, playing at a friend's house, twenty-six-year old Mavis didn't have any interruptions to worry about. Sure, she loved Tad, but being a single mother could be exhausting. She cherished these few minutes alone before she had to pick up her son, feed him dinner, and try to convince him that going to bed early was a good idea.

Mavis pushed her wet hair out of her eyes and looked up toward the molded plastic shelf in the corner of the tub for her shampoo. Instead, her eyes were drawn to the small window at the top of the bathroom wall, because a man's face was centered in the metal frame, his unsmiling eyes fixed on her.

Mavis screamed and grabbed the shower curtain to shield her body. She stumbled onto the bathroom floor, nearly falling in the slick water that cascaded from her wet skin and pooled at her feet. She made a dash for the bathroom door. Some instinct made her grab a towel with one hand while she wrenched the bathroom door open with the other. She fled down the hall, wrapping the towel around her as she went, and shut herself in her bedroom.

Mavis grabbed the phone and pushed herself into the back of her closet, crouching on the floor as she tried to dial her neighbors, Hillary and Rich. Although she had her friends' phone number memorized, it took a couple of tries before she got it right. They'd been friends ever since her mother, who was a minister, had married Hillary and Rich in a casual outdoor ceremony in a Washington park in 2002.

The phone rang. It rang again. Mavis was starting to panic by the time Hillary picked up the phone and said, "Hello?"

"Someone's looking in my bathroom window," Mavis said, trembling so badly that her voice shook.

"We'll be right there."

In less than a minute, Mavis heard the door of her trailer house open, and Hillary call out, "Mavis?" Mavis was grateful she'd given them a key in case of emergencies.

While Hillary stood guard, Mavis pulled on some sweats and went outside with her neighbors to investigate.

The two women followed Rich around the side of the house toward the bathroom window. They halted and looked up at the rectangle of glass that sat a good eight feet above their heads. Unless the peeping tom had the dimensions of Goliath, he would have had to stand on something in order to see in.

"Seen any pro basketball players hanging around lately?" Rich asked.

"Rich!" Hillary reprimanded him. "That's not funny!" She put a reassuring arm around Mavis's shoulders.

Rich scuffed his toe into the spongy soil typical of the northwest United States. "Well, I don't see any sign of a ladder or chair or anything set up here," he said. "There aren't even any footprints."

"There are now," Hillary said, glaring at the divot that Rich had made with his work boot.

Rich conducted a more thorough search, but finally even Hillary had to admit that there were no signs of anyone having been in a spot where they could have looked into Mavis's window.

The couple helped Mavis to calm down. Rich did a sweep of her home, assuring her that no one was hiding inside. Before they left, the couple insisted that Mavis could call them for help at any time.

A few days later, Mavis walked into her bathroom and was nearly startled out of her socks when through the curtain she saw the silhouette of a man standing under the shower head in her bathtub. Acting on a sudden bold surge of anger battling with fear, she grabbed the curtain and yanked it open.

The tub was empty.

As much as she may have wanted to, Mavis couldn't avoid her bathroom forever. One night she went in to use it before going to bed. After she sat down, she was unnerved to feel a hand descend onto her shoulder. She jerked her head around to see who was there but only saw her shoulder, even though she could feel the weight and shape of a hand resting there.

The next day, Rich and Hillary stopped by. While Mavis started telling Hillary about the strange incident the night before, Rich excused himself to use her bathroom. He locked the door, sat down, and was startled to feel a hand descend onto his shoulder. He gave a little yelp and whipped his head around, his fist gripping the handle of the plunger that sat next to the commode, but no one was there.

Rich pulled himself together and burst out of the bathroom door. "You won't believe what just happened."

Mavis believed him.

After Mavis and Rich compared notes on the unwanted bathroom visitor, Hillary made an announcement. "Hey, Rich, I'm going to take Mavis out for lunch. She needs a break. Will you watch Tad for her?"

Rich took one look at Mavis's anxious face and agreed.

After the women left, Rich watched TV from a spot on the couch, since the rocking chair was taken up by two heavy boxes stacked on top of one another. As soon as the program was over, Rich told Tad that he was stepping out for a smoke. Tad followed him outside and drove his toy trucks on the porch.

"A few moments later, I went back inside and saw the rocking chair totally tipped over, with the two heavy boxes also tipped over on the floor," Rich said. There was no one else at home, and he couldn't think of any logical explanation for it.

When Mavis got home, Rich told her what had happened. Not long after that, Mavis and Tad moved away.

Rich and Hillary didn't seem to be as put off by the ghost as Mavis was. In fact, when they noticed in the paper that this "haunted' trailer was up for rent, they talked about renting it. The only reason they decided not to? Rich said, "It doesn't have any place to put a washer and dryer like the apartment complex we're moving into does."

Carol lived with her husband and three sons in a tiny 700 square foot house in Midvale, Utah. From the living room couch, it was easy to see the bathroom doorway and short hall that led to the two bedrooms.

One day, when all three boys were playing in their room, Carol saw a little boy run from the bathroom right into the master bedroom.

"The boys were not allowed in our room without permission," Carol said. "They all knew the rule, and they all abided by it."

Carol got up to reprimand the son who had just made a wrong turn, but when she went into her bedroom, there was no one there.

She checked the room across the hall. Her sons glanced up from their play, but not one of them even spared her a "Hi, Mom." She knew it wasn't them she'd seen.

That wasn't the last time the mysterious boy ran from the bathroom.

"It happened all the time," Carol said. "He looked just like my boys. He wasn't transparent or anything."

Carol still checked her room whenever she saw him disappear through her door, but she never found anyone.

Inevitably, Carol's sons grew bigger and taller. Strangely enough, so did the ghost.

"He grew up with my boys," Carol said of the five and a half years they lived in the house. "He looked just like a person. He looked like one of our boys. He was always running, always from the bathroom to my room, and we only saw him from the back."

In a separate haunting in Kansas, the ghost would only bother the family in the bathroom, and then only when the children's friends came over to play.

Their mother, Anita, happened to have long hair, which the ghost liked to flick while Anita was using the bathroom.

The ghost also liked to flush the toilet whether the person was ready or not.

One day, when Anita once again felt her hair flip up in the back from unseen hands, she got fed up.

"Do you know what?" she said out loud to the empty room. "You never bother us until the kids' friends come over, and then you act up, so I want you to stop it right now!"

And it did.

The Guilty Ghost

Failure to forgive oneself can hurt in more ways than one

It was nine PM on a chill autumn night in 1989. Christine Savage was alone in the old Carnegie Library, finishing up some paperwork so that she could lock up and go home.

Without any preliminary warning, a "thump" sounded behind her. Startled, Christine spun around in her chair to see who was there. There was no one.

"Excuse me," she called out in a voice that sounded braver than she felt. "It's closing time."

Silence.

Christine began to wonder if she'd really heard anything at all. She pushed herself up from her chair and walked down the length of the bookshelves. She didn't hear or see a soul.

When she turned the corner, she stopped and stared at a book lying on the floor. All of the books were shelved a generous three inches from the edge. The space that this book had filled was conspicuously empty. Christine found herself wondering, *did that really happen?*

After a cautious glance around, Christine bent over and picked up the book. The title was *The Seventh Winter.*

A thrill ran down her spine. She could think of no other explanation for what had just happened except that there was a ghost involved. "I figured that I'd been working here for about two years," Christine said. "So I thought that maybe by the seventh winter of my employment, I might find out what was going on."

Christine opened the cover, then turned the flyleaf. The dedication was simple. *For Barbara,* it said. "I eventually figured out that the ghost must be named Barbara," Christine said.

Five years later, on a cold winter day, Christine walked over to the library elevator and pushed the button. As soon as the doors opened, her eyes zeroed in on a scrap of paper on the elevator floor. She picked it up and unfolded it. There were three words printed there: *The Seventh Winter.*

The falling book was not the only paranormal incident that Christine experienced. "I've been working on a bottom shelf and had a book fall on my head. I've heard magazine pages turning and not thought anything about it because people sit in the magazine section and do that, but then I realized that no one was back there. I've heard laughter, a girl's laughter, and nobody's been here." After a moment of thought, Christine added, "It's pleasant laughter."

The first time Christine actually saw the ghost was when she was supervising a teenage girl named Amy who was working off a library fine. "The rule when you're working here is that you can't bring any friends with you," Christine explained. "Amy knew the rule before she asked me if she could clean out a downstairs closet. She was a good self-starter, so I said she could."

Amy had been working for twenty-five or thirty minutes when Christine went downstairs to see how she was doing. "I was on the stairs when I saw a young girl go running by and duck into the corner room."

Sure that she had caught Amy breaking the rule, and that she'd just witnessed her friend running for cover as soon as she heard Christine's feet on the stairs, Christine parked herself beside the doorway of the closet where she had a clear view of the corner room. Christine made some small talk, waiting for Amy to admit that she had a friend hiding down there, but Amy was all innocence. She never darted a single glance in the direction that her friend had disappeared.

"Finally, I figured I'd just go get whoever it was," Christine said. "I walked over to the door and opened it, but there was no one in there."

Amy didn't seem surprised by her actions. "Amy told me that she often second-guessed people, and that she could read minds a little bit," Christine said. "I believed her, because of the ghost girl."

There have been other times when Christine was working alone in the library when it was closed, just so she could catch up on her work. "I've heard footsteps walk past the front of the desk," Christine said. "They go out the doors and down the steps toward the basement. One day I followed them just to see where she was going, but once I got to the basement, I got chills and goose bumps and ran back upstairs."

Christine also saw the ghost once on the main floor of the library, standing about six feet in from a side door that has a window. "She looked kind of like Jessica Lang in the *O Pioneers* movie."

Another librarian, who didn't know of the encounters, told Christine that she'd seen a young woman through the window of the same door, only on the outside. When she went to let her in, there was no one there. She did mention that the young woman had looked sort of odd.

"How odd?" Christine wanted to know.

"Well, she had her hair up, not like people wear today, and the neck of her shirt seemed sort of, well, old fashioned."

Christine got the video *O Pioneers* off the shelf. "Did she look anything like this?"

The librarian's eyes went wide. "Yes, she looked a lot like that."

For a time, the library kept a cat with the idea that the patrons could sit and read with a cat curled up on their lap. Unfortunately, the cat would rather extend a hostile claw than a friendly paw to most of the patrons. He liked Christine well enough but was stand-offish at best with almost everyone else.

Then Christine began to notice the cat behaving oddly. "The cat used to sit on the table and act like he was getting petted. He'd arch his neck and close his eyes and lean in toward something I couldn't see. I wonder if he was her pet." Christine paused in thought. "Then the cat died, so maybe he's her pet now, but I haven't seen a ghost cat."

One lady who said she was a channeler, which is someone who claims to have the ability to communicate with spirits, visited the library once. After spending some time trying to communicate with Barbara, she said that the ghost girl comes in the autumn and always around Halloween. She also mentioned something about a little brother, and some guilt associated with the ghost.

"I don't think the little brother's here," Christine said. "I think something happened to Barbara's little brother, and she's either waiting for him to come back, or she feels guilty about what happened to him. It feels like she's a teenager about fourteen years old.

"Maybe Halloween came to be because lots of people noticed that strange things were happening then," Christine mused. "That's the exact opposite of May first, which marks the traditional festival time of growing things. I wonder if it's an old Celtic thing, and there's a reason they picked that time is because people who had died started showing up."

Christine says she can go all summer and not have anything happen, but in the autumn, she starts to see and hear things.

Christine said that her mother, who passed away a few years ago, also comes back at Halloween. "But she plays tricks. Last year I had this meeting in the city. After I got there, I pulled out my lipstick and put it on. It's one I wear all the time, no darker than just regular pink. After the meetings were over, I went in the bathroom and stared in the mirror. My lips were hot pink, the ugliest lipstick I had ever seen. It's the kind my mom used to wear. That was her favorite color. I said, 'Don't you do that, I'm trying to make a good impression on these people!' Mom was a character."

One night, Christine was telling a library board member about the ghost. He said, "I'd like to have an encounter with her."

Just then, they heard a book flop down on the bookcase. It could have fallen anyway, but it sure fell at an opportune time.

"That's happened several times with different people," Christine said. "One of the funniest ones that happened is when my old schoolmate, Olivia, and I were working together on a class reunion."

Christine asked Olivia to help her carry some supplies back into the library when the reunion was over. It was a dark evening in May, around ten PM, and Christine confessed that she didn't always like to be in the library alone at night. When Olivia asked why, Christine told her.

"I don't believe in stuff like that," Olivia said.

When everything was put away, Christine drove Olivia home.

About ten or fifteen minutes later, Christine's phone rang. It was Olivia. "This isn't funny," she said.

"What's not funny?"

There was a moment of silence, then Olivia said, "Did you go straight home after you dropped me off?"

"Yes."

Another moment of silence. "Then you're not ringing my doorbell every time I'm getting ready to go to bed?"

It wasn't Christine.

"I've noticed that people who challenge her existence and claim they don't believe in her almost force Barbara to prove to them that she's around," Christine said. "But she'll never bother people who are genuinely afraid of her."

One of the part-time high school workers was scared

half to death at the idea of seeing or hearing a ghost. Barbara never had anything to do with her.

Before she'd heard any of the stories, another high school girl told Christine that there was a poltergeist in the library. This girl made periodic attempts to contact Barbara through the library computers. "I don't think she ever did, though," said Christine.

Barbara has never hurt anyone. "I've seen her, heard her, and felt her," Christine said. In the evening, when Christine is all alone and leaving the library, she often tells Barbara good-night.

One evening at closing time, Sheila Smith and her daughter Mary Michelle Smith were the last ones in the library. "Have you had any more experiences with your friend, the ghost?" Sheila asked.

"Well, nothing recently, but it seems that as soon as someone brings up the subject, something happens," Christine said.

They got into a conversation about moving on to the other side after this life. Sheila mentioned how she'd heard that sometimes ghosts need to move on, but they don't realize they're dead.

"I guess Barbara has never heard that before," Christine quipped.

"So I cupped my mouth with my hands and said, 'Honest, you can go, you can move on. Can you hear me?'" Sheila said.

In the brief silence that followed, the floor creaked. "Did you hear that?" Christine asked.

Sheila looked around at the empty stacks of books. She leaned in toward Christine and asked, "Has this building always been a library?"

"Yes, but there used to be another building on this same lot," Christine said. She moved a few steps toward a row of old photographs hanging on the wall and pointed to one. "The old council house was torn down so the library could be built sometime in the early 1900s."

One story that's been told is that the old two-story council house was once used to lock up several Indian men in the latter part of the 1800s. An adolescent Indian girl, a plucky daughter of one of the prisoners, snuck in and helped them escape. Unfortunately for them, they were discovered in mid-flight and shot down.

"Do you want me to show you where I feel her most?" Christine took Sheila and Mary over to a window. She leaned over the wide window ledge and looked out. "It's as though the ghost stands and watches out this window all the time." Then she stepped back.

Sheila moved in to take her place. "I felt the skin crawl on the back of my neck," Sheila said.

Nine-year-old Mary had a turn at the window. "When I feel like there is somebody unseen close to me, I can feel my fingers tingling like I might have gone through them or something," Mary said. "When I looked out the upstairs window, I felt that feeling. I've felt spirits around before, like in our house. I'm calm about it, but sometimes I feel like something's going on but I don't know what."

"There's another place where I often feel her," said Christine, and led the way to the basement.

Before following her mother through the door, Mary glanced over her shoulder. "When we went downstairs, I heard a creak where nobody was standing over by where they keep the videos, and I thought that meant she might be following us downstairs," she said.

Once in the basement, Christine walked over to a railing that bordered a ramp, which had been installed for handicapped access. "When I saw her once before, she walked over to this railing and then walked through it," Christine explained.

Then Christine stopped dead still. In a quiet voice, she said, "She's right here next to me. Can you feel her?"

"I could feel a difference in the air," Sheila said. "I moved over next to Christine and immediately I could feel other thoughts in my head. Christine didn't know that anything was happening inside my head, but took my silence to mean that I wasn't paying attention."

"Doesn't it feel cold to you?" Christine wanted to know.

"It was cold where Mrs. Savage said it was," Mary said. "I felt like there was more than one spirit person. I could feel a difference in the personalities."

Sheila said, "I noticed that the spot I was standing was cold, but I was paying more attention to the thoughts in my mind. They were abstract, they weren't like having a conversation. The ideas that came to me were of not being able to leave that building. In my mind, I asked her why. The impression came to me that it was because of her little brother."

Just then, Christine moved away from the area and into another room. Sheila followed and asked, "Was there anything that happened in the library involving a little boy?"

"Oh, this is weird," Christine said. She wrapped her arms around her elbows. "You just gave me goose bumps. I've heard this before." Christine then told Sheila about the channeler who had been in the library earlier.

"I continued to feel the presence in the room near us," Sheila said. "I kept getting vague, abstract ideas swirling around in my mind. I was sending out thoughts for her to let go and progress. She was saying, 'I can't, I can't, I can't.' And I was trying to reassure her in my thoughts that she would really be a whole lot happier if she let go of here and moved on, that it would be wonderful and glorious. I got the impression of a distraught teenager that hadn't followed through, and because of it, some traumatic thing happened. Maybe she's punishing herself. She didn't feel worthy to move on. I got the feeling that she didn't think she was worthy to see Jesus or to go to Heaven.

"Then we walked out into the hall and the hangers on

the little coat rack started swinging as though someone was bumping them."

Mary saw it too. "The hangers moved like somebody was taking a coat off the hangers or two coats off the hangers," she said.

Christine stared at the strangely animated hangers and said, "You're not leaving before I do."

When Christine hurried to put things away and close up the library, the drawers on her desk kept popping open, and the floor creaked as though someone were walking on it.

"It was a perfect day because of the storminess," Sheila said, referring to the idea that stormy weather can enhance the ability to interact with spirits. "And it was a full moon, too."

The three of them went outside and walked around the south side of the library. Christine stopped and looked up at the window that the ghost seemed to favor. There appeared to be a faint mist of white staring back at them.

But then, it could have been the reflection of the storm clouds playing hide and seek with the moon.

Lost Boy

Who is the ghost boy playing hide and seek and looking for a big sister?

In the year 2000, fourteen-year-old Adelaide started seeing the ghost of a little boy.

"It started when we had our dining room table set up in the front room," Adelaide said. "It looked like the boy was about ten. He had short, dark hair. I'd see him hide behind the table, then he'd peek out at me, and run away—stuff like little kids do. At night I'd walk through the front room, and he'd be standing there. When I went upstairs, he'd be standing at the top. Once I was in the kitchen and thought I saw my younger brother in there with me. I went into the living room and there was my brother on the couch. When I looked back into the kitchen, the other boy was gone."

Adelaide was finally able to communicate with the ghost through a dream. "I was dreaming of a white room. The boy was sitting there crying. I asked him what he wanted. He said that he wanted my big sister, Rose Marie. But Rose Marie had moved away to college by then."

Shortly after Adelaide's dream, her mother saw the little ghost boy and asked him what he wanted. When he said, "Rose Marie," Mom told him that she didn't live there anymore.

Rose Marie says that the ghost was around even before he started playing hide and seek with Adelaide. "He was here before I left," she said. "I had a dream about him standing in my doorway, and he spoke to me, but I couldn't understand him. I picked him up. I physically felt him in my arms, and I took him to Mom. She could understand him. After she talked to him, I set him on the back porch and closed the door. Then I woke up. There was definitely someone in the room when I woke up. It wasn't terrifying or scary. It was more that I wanted to know what it was all about and who it was. I had a billion questions."

The most recent visit of the mysterious ghost boy was in 2004. "I was coming to visit the family for Memorial Day. Adelaide had gone up to my old room and saw the ghost boy sitting on my bed and crying," Rose Marie said. When Adelaide asked what was wrong, the ghost boy said he wanted Rose Marie. Adelaide told him that she'd be there the next day. The boy calmed down, quit crying, and faded away.

No one in the family has seen him since.

Voices in the Hall

Church halls are supposed to be quiet after 10 PM.

Jay told a strange story he'd heard about an eerie event that happened in the mid 1950s. It seems that some men finished a late night meeting on the second floor of a church. When they left the room and started down the staircase, they were astonished to see the devil appear on the stairs before them, refusing to let them pass. "They had a little discussion, and the devil got cast out," Jay remembered.

In the years since that unsettling event, Jay has become a church man himself. In the early 1990s, Jay found himself in meetings held inside the same church that had the enviousless distinction of being the one the devil had visited. Jay's meetings were normally held in the evening after regular church services. Although those in attendance liked to get things done as soon as possible, sometimes the meetings ran late.

"Several times we'd be in there after 10 o'clock," Jay said. "We'd be in the office and hear voices in the hall. We'd get up and look, and there'd never be anyone there."

It was puzzling, to say the least. But the bodiless voices weren't the only disturbance. Sometimes it sounded as though someone were moving around just outside the closed door. "We'd hear footsteps in the hall," Jay said. "We'd get up and look again, and there was never anyone there."

Hearing footsteps and voices in the empty church when the outside doors were locked didn't happen every time a meeting ran late. But it happened often enough that there's no doubt in Jay's mind that something bizarre was going on. He knew he didn't imagine it, because other people in the room heard it, too. "It happened numerous times, and it was always after 10 o'clock before the ghost or whoever it was came out," Jay said.

Does he think the devil returned after dark to stalk the halls, looking for unwary souls to steal?

"We never felt like it was evil; it was just unusual," Jay explained.

Another reason it probably wasn't the devil, even if you dismissed the story that he'd been cast out of the building, is that Jay is certain that what he heard outside the closed door "was more than one being."

Even though Jay doesn't think the voices and footsteps are evil, he still prefers to avoid the ghostly visitors.

One night Jay was in the church with Matt when he told Matt that they would definitely be through before 10 PM.

"Why?" Matt asked. "What happens at ten o'clock?"

"Then it's someone else's time to use the building," Jay said.

Wyatt Earp Followed Her Home

Sometimes ghosts can sense when mortals might help.

Tombstone, Arizona, carries a reputation for a lot of ghostly activity. Three of Sara Gray's friends encountered some legendary spirits while visiting there. The freinds referred to the spirits, Wyatt Earp, Doc Holiday, and Bat Masterson, as "The Three Amigos."

The Amigos followed their mortal acquaintances back to Mesa, where Sara met up with them at a restaurant.

"If any of my friends referred to the Amigos as cowboys, the Amigos would correct them and I would hear them say, 'We're not cowboys, we're gunslingers and gamblers,'" Sara said. "I knew they were around, but I didn't really want to focus on them.

"About four days later, I went over to a friend's house and we were talking about Wyatt Earp and Bat Masterson. After I left, I went over to a bookstore. I would take one book off a shelf to look at, and five other books would fall on the floor. Everywhere I went, things kept falling off the shelves. I thought, *that is not me, someone else is here.* I wasn't scared; I just thought it was weird."

Sara went home but continued to feel a presence with her for the rest of the day. "In my car, I felt a presence beside me. I finally tuned in to it and found out it was Wyatt Earp. He'd been earthbound for a long time, and he'd had some tragic things happen in his life. I figured out that he wanted some help in getting over the death of his first wife. Her death is what started him on a dark path. He was still grieving over her, and wasn't with her because she was a good woman. He wasn't in the place where she was, so I helped him clear some of those emotions out of his system. He was happier and in a place of more light when he left."

Why did he come to her for help? "Somehow, I know that spirits can tell when somebody can help them, feel them, or see them," Sara said.

Wyatt Earp visited Sara again about six months after that, when she was with one of her friends. "We were talking about him and he showed up. Speaking about people is stronger than thinking of them. Words are vibration, and they're powerful. We'd been goofing around, talking about the Wyatt Earp movies that had been made with Kevin Costner and Kurt Russell. Wyatt Earp came along and said that he liked Kevin better because he was better looking. We got a good laugh about that.

"Wyatt had a favorite horse that had been shot. He wanted my help to clear his grief from losing his horse. It seems to me like he's feeling a lot happier."

Sara explains her affinity to sense spirits this way: "I believe that all gifts are from God. He has given me the gift to feel spirits and communicate with them somewhat in order to help them and for no other reason. I have always been sensitive to energies, good and bad. I do not call people to me or act as a medium. But at times, spirit people will just show up, and if the Lord wants me to do something to help them, then I do. If not, I ask them to leave."

The Livery Stable

Who's still inhabiting the century-old stable?

The Blackfoot Canvas Company in Blackfoot, Idaho, is housed in part of an old livery stable, built in 1881. Kimberley Huffaker's grandfather started the canvas business in 1960. "We build tents and tepees," Kimberley said with a laugh. "So in a way, we're still in the eighteenth century."

Having spent several years in one wing of the old building, Kimberley has had some firsthand accounts with the ghost who lives there. "Our ghost is a regular visitor, but he doesn't visit all the time," Kimberley said. "My family's had him visit on and off over the years. Sometimes he's more active than others."

One of the things the ghost is blamed for is pushing open the garage door that was installed back in 1904 when concrete was first poured. "We used to have this big, heavy garage door with a double lock," Kimberley said. "You had to push a button and turn a handle to make it unlock. Sometimes when I was sure it was locked, it would just raise up by itself. You had to watch it, because it would do it while you were working by it." Sometimes when Kimberley or one of her family was in one of the other two sections of the old livery stable, they'd come back to their shop only to find the locked door raised, but nobody was there.

That was just the start. "The front door was originally

a double door with glass in it," Kimberley said. "Once in awhile we'd hear it open and close and the bell would go off, but there'd be nobody there. A couple of times the wind would blow the door open but then it would close, but a door can't close by itself against the wind."

It wasn't only family who witnessed the ghostly events. "We had one gal named Rachel who worked with us for thirty years," Kimberley said. "She started working with my grandfather and my mother. Rachel was sitting in here working with me one day and we heard the front door open and we both looked at each other. It was a Saturday and we weren't officially open, but we had some work to catch up on. All of a sudden, we smelled Chinese food. It wafted right though the room and went off into the next bay." There was no one there except the two women. At least, no one they could see.

One night, Kimberley took her dog to the shop. "I was working on a paint job about 10:30 at night," Kimberley said. "My dog was in the middle bay in the main livery stable part. I heard him in there barking little barks, then growling, then barking, then growling. I called him, but he didn't turn around. He backed up toward me, keeping up that strange, angry bark. I finally called Mom and let her listen to him." For about twenty minutes, Kimberley's dog stared right in front of him, in that four-legged stance dogs use when they challenge an intruder, his back curled up in defense.

After Kimberley hung up from talking to her mother, she had an idea. "Maybe it's time to call it a good night," she said out loud.

The dog kept barking, so Kimberley spoke louder. "Maybe it's time to call it a good night. I'll just wash up my brushes and go home."

Ten seconds later, the dog stopped barking.

"The dog knew someone was there," Kimberley said. "I think the ghost is just living here."

Kimberley has come to the conclusion that the ghost feels that his time is when the store is supposed to be closed. "I've had the distinct feeling that at 10:30 PM, it's the ghost's time," Kimberley said.

But what can you do about jobs that have deadlines and require overtime hours?

"One time, at about three in the morning, we were still working on some stuff that had to be done," Kimberley said. "My sister, Katrina, and her husband, Roger, came down to give us a hand. Roger thought it was creepy in the middle of the night, because the building settles and breathes. We had material stacked in one end of the room and some webbing sitting flat on a stack. When Roger walked past the stack, this roll of webbing flipped over and landed on the floor at his heels."

There was no visible cause for the webbing to flip itself over and land on the floor.

"We stayed until morning to get the job done," Kimberley said. "But Roger said, 'I'm not working here at night anymore.'"

Roger named the ghost Elmo after a man who worked with Kimberley's grandpa, and was older than Grandpa himself. But Kimberley's pretty sure the ghost isn't really the deceased Elmo. "I think the ghost is older than that," Kimberley said. "I think he was prior to the canvas shop. I think he was part of the original livery stable and not someone in this part of the century."

Early on, Kimberley's family discovered straw piled in the loft above the former stall area where the horses used to wait for their riders. Although some of it has been used, they left most of it there for the ghost. From the evidence scattered about, it appears that the hayloft was the living quarters for at least one person. "I found some old newspapers from 1918–1922 when it was still a livery stable," Kimberley said. "I found pitchfork holes in some of the papers. I also found some 1904 whiskey bottles."

In 1995, a man in his 80s came into the canvas company and told Kimberley that he'd learned to ride his bike in the livery stable. When he got a little older, he worked nights in the stable. If a doctor had a night call, Kimberley's visitor was the young whippersnapper who got the buggy ready. There had to be somebody there around the clock, so whoever was working at the time, along with the occasional man who stabled his horse overnight, would sleep in the loft.

Although many people have made the livery their temporary home during its history, Kimberley doesn't think they're all haunting it. "I think there's just one ghost," she said. "He's not a radical. He doesn't interfere. He doesn't hurt us. He's not vicious. You just know he's around. Sometimes I talk to him. He comes and goes. You'll hear him more in the summer or fall, but if I know there's activity while I'm hanging around at night, I'll tell him I'm here to work and I'll be there that evening."

Does Kimberley ever think of moving the canvas company to avoid the ghost?

"He doesn't frighten me, so I don't think much about it," she said.

The Tromper and the Playful Ghost

Two ghosts inhabit this dwelling,
one restless, one playful

When Tery moved from California to Mayfield, Utah, she planned to live by herself, just down the road from her parents' house. She bought an interesting old amalgamated structure that came complete with an unusual history.

One part of her new home was a two-story rock schoolhouse built at the end of the 1800s. This was where she encountered her first ghost.

After clearing out one of her moving boxes, Tery glanced at the rest that she still had to go through, and decided that she'd store them in the attic when they were unpacked. She climbed up the steep attic stairs to have a look around. The room was completely empty, except for dirt and scraps of paper on the floor.

Getting sidetracked as so many of us do, Tery thought that it would be a good idea to spend a few minutes cleaning up the attic before she stored anything there. "I started pushing the dirt into a pile with my foot. Then I decided to go get a broom," Tery said.

Leaving the small pile of debris, Tery made her way downstairs and picked up the broom. When she returned to the attic, she stopped dead at the top of the stairs, gazing in frank disbelief at the spot where she'd been working.

"There was an old cribbage game sitting in the middle

of the dirt," Tery said. "The only reason I knew it was a cribbage game is because I played it once in the 1980s."

With the hair rising on the back of her neck, Tery glanced into the shadowy corners of the attic.

Empty.

But where had the game come from? And who had put it there? Tery was the only person in the house.

"When I asked the former owners if they'd ever heard of any weird things going on in the place, they said, 'Yeah, we have a ghost. We think there are two.'"

The cribbage game ghost is rumored to be an old school marm who used to teach in the schoolhouse. "I haven't seen her, but the former owners have," Tery said.

Once she had some idea of who may have offered her the game, Tery said, "I had the feeling that she was saying to me, 'Girl, you need a rest.'"

Tery took the game to her parents' house and showed it to her mother. "There were some pencil markings and things on it," Tery said. "It looked pretty old."

After hearing Tery's story, her mother said, "Well, does that mean she wants to play with you? Why don't you go up there start playing; make a move and see if she moves a piece, too."

"Oh, no," Tery laughed. "I'm not going there."

But when Tery returned to her house, she soon met another ghost.

"The school marm acts differently than the one over there," Tery said, indicating the restaurant portion of her house with her thumb.

The restaurant is made up of a single story section salvaged from the World War II Topaz Internment Camp in Utah's West Desert, where displaced Japanese Americans were confined during the uneasy war years.

The original reason the barrack building was moved in the 1950s was for it to become a hat manufacturing plant. When the bottom dropped out of the hat industry, the former barracks evolved into a restaurant called "The Old Bonnet Factory."

Tery planned to keep the restaurant running while living in the old schoolhouse. She delved into a vigorous remodeling spree, spending hours scraping off old wallpaper that boasted a rather annoying hat motif. In a burst of whimsy, Tery decided to re-name the restaurant "Hats off Cafe."

"It was while I was working to open the restaurant that the second ghost appeared," Tery said. "The tromper came late at night when I was cleaning the place. He tromps back and forth in the restaurant."

Tery didn't talk about the tromper to her employees, but they soon found out for themselves. "I hadn't mentioned him to anyone who worked there," Tery said, "But my waitress was closing up and cleaning late one night and kept hearing him."

Tery got used to the tromper pacing back and forth, back and forth, covering the length of the old barracks from one end to the other. "One day I yelled, 'If you're going to tromp back and forth, then get a broom!'" Tery said.

She's not sure who it is or why he's so restless. "Maybe it's someone from the internment camp or someone who used to work in the hat factory."

Tery has since closed her restaurant but still lives in the building. She's quite content to share her dwelling. After all, the tromper and the playful ghost were there first.

Little Sister

Even after death, this ghost never outgrew her love for Christmas.

When a ghost hunter heard about all the ghosts Carol has seen, he admitted that he'd never actually seen a ghost. "It's commonplace for me," Carol said.

A couple of incidents were only slight brushes with the paranormal, such as the time her 21-year-old son walked past a captain's wheel that decorated a spot next to the front door. The wheel was hung with beads that began swinging wildly as soon as he drew alongside them. Spooked, the young man hurried to tell his parents. Carol and her husband got to the front room in time to see the beads moving back and forth.

"When they stopped, we tried to make them move. We got really close and blew on them, but it didn't work," Carol said.

On a different day, Carol's peripheral vision spied a pair of legs walk past. She didn't look up, assuming that the legs clad in Levis and battered old tennis shoes belonged to her son. They moved from the kitchen to the laundry room and back again, then out of sight.

Only then did Carol realize her son wasn't home. She checked just to be sure. She was alone.

When Carol worked as a Certified Nursing Assistant, she saw two different mists move down a hospital corridor and turn a corner. One mist was dark, and one was light.

Although she saw them at different times, they both followed the same path.

It was only when she and her husband rented a house next to the railroad tracks in Draper, Utah, in 1985, that she saw a more substantial spirit.

"It was an old farmhouse," Carol said. "There were transoms over the windows, and a swinging door that separated the kitchen from the living room."

Carol and her husband rented from a couple of elderly brothers named Jay and Roy who were in their 70s. The two men had grown up in the house, which they turned into a rental after their father died.

Carol and her husband unpacked and put things away, arranging their living room furniture into a cozy "L" shape. They set up their Christmas tree and decorated it with the help of their enthusiastic five-year-old son.

One cold December day, Carol pushed on the swinging door from the kitchen side to go into the living room. "I saw a young girl hovering over the couch, facing the Christmas tree," Carol said. "She had curly hair and a beautiful lacy dress. I was looking over her left shoulder." The ghost was all white: her skin, her hair, and even her dress, which shaded to soft, luminescent gray in the folds.

As the door opened, the ghost girl glided away from it, never taking her eyes off the decorated tree. She didn't move her feet; she just floated away. As soon as Carol had the door all the way open, the ghost was positioned about five feet from the couch. Then she disappeared.

The next time Carol saw Jay, she told him about the ghostly sighting. After describing the pretty spirit girl, she noticed Jay's face drain to an unhealthy pallor.

Alarmed, Carol asked, "What is it?"

"That was my little sister," Jay whispered. "She died of rheumatic fever in this house when she was twelve years old.

Shadow People

One is a man, the other, a girl in pigtails;
only their shadows are seen.

In the summer of 2003, fourteen-year-old Chelcey Weber's family changed towns and moved into an older home. At around midnight, Chelcey was in her new room listening to her radio when all of a sudden, the station went fuzzy. "I saw the shadows and thought they were my parents," Chelcey said. "I even yelled my mom's name."

Although there were two figures in Chelcey's room, they were most certainly not her parents. One was a tall man, and the other a young girl with pigtails. There were no details of her visitor's features, only the shapes of their bodies in shadow. "It wasn't like any of the ghost stories I ever heard of," Chelcey said. "It was like I could see their body shapes, but where their eyes were supposed to be, you could see through, and where their mouths were you could see through them. I was really scared and I laid back down, thinking, *this is just my imagination.* I looked up again and they were gone."

Chelcey told her mother what she'd seen, but she had no intention of telling her older sister or five-year-old brother about it. She didn't want to scare them.

But the shadow man had no such qualms.

"One time, my brother was sleeping in my sister's room and he thought he saw something, so he peeked over the covers. He saw the tall man and he described it as exactly what I saw, and I'd never said a word to him."

Although she only saw the girl with pigtails once, Chelcey has seen the shadow man several times. She's pretty sure her baby boy has seen him too. "My son will sometimes wake up crying, but he's not teething or anything. He just wakes up screaming. That's unusual for him."

One night, Chelcey was getting a bottle for her baby. She turned the corner from the kitchen to go upstairs and thought she saw something. She looked back to see the shadow ghost standing in the corner. "I didn't dare walk around at night anymore," Chelcey said, "and I never saw the ghost again."

Sometimes the light switches would flip off and on. "It was scary because we didn't know who did it," Chelcey said.

Chelcey's mother asked the lady they'd bought the house from about the ghosts, but she didn't know anything about them. Although Chelcey was curious and wanted to research more about who the nocturnal visitors could be, enough was enough. Chelcey's parents had the house blessed. "Every now and then I look for the ghosts, but I can't see them anymore," Chelcey said. "Nothing has happened since then."

The Handyman Ghost

This former murder scene comes with the last kind of ghost you'd expect: a helpful one.

Maurine Smith was a single mother with two children when she left Las Vegas to start over. As soon as she saw the old two-story rental house, she knew it was where she wanted to live. "It just opened its arms up to us," Maurine said. "It needed us. When we first got this house, it had been lived in for eight years by college students." Apparently, none of the students had ever taken a course in house maintenance 101.

Maurine is one of those people who has an affinity to tune into feelings. "I was working on a broken door one day, and I 'felt' the house say, 'My name is Rose.'" Smith said, "She needed someone to love her and clean her up."

Maurine talked to the landlord about needed repairs. "Basically, when we talked about approval, she said, 'When you do something major, check with me, but anything else, go ahead.'"

Since she was on her own, Smith found it necessary to learn home repairs. Fortunately, she had a ghost that was willing to teach her.

"The neighbors told me that there had been a murder here back in the 1930s," Smith said. She was curious about the details and finally decided to look up the story. "I went back through the *Sanpete County Messenger.* Then one day it came to me to check the cemetery records, and that's where I found it."

A local banker had been bludgeoned to death in the kitchen of the very home that Maurine now lived in. While following the newspaper account of the trial, Smith discovered that the banker's daughter and her boyfriend were suspected of killing the old man for his money. It ended up that the boyfriend went to prison and the daughter got off.

"The newspaper account said the banker was killed with a faggot of wood from the apple tree out back," Smith said. "Once he was dead, the guy doused him with oil and tried to light him on fire. The fire went up into the attic, and the bricks up there are still scorched."

In spite of the tragic account she discovered, Smith says, "I never felt any negative energy from that event."

The ghost that looked over her shoulder when she wielded a hammer was a helpful one.

"The times I'd sense the presence of this person were when I was working on something. I'd get the impression to go look somewhere for what I needed, and I had ideas that I never would have thought of, like using a drawer from an old dresser for parts to fix something. It was nice to have the company."

Smith ended up running wires and water pipes as well as doing carpentry work. One day, Smith was trying to figure out the next step in building a partition wall. All of a sudden, she got the distinct impression of a man standing by her, just to one side and in back of her. "It's not like I saw anybody, but just that I felt something," she said. "It was dimensional, like the perception that you have of seeing a whole person. He was around six feet tall, slender, with a wiry build, but not skinny. He was quiet and gentle. I got the feeling that he was curious about what I was doing."

Smith described the encounter as a positive experience. "There're too many coincidences, blessings, and miracles that happen to deny the existence of spirits that are here."

Smith's handyman ghost didn't confine himself to overseeing the in-house projects, either. One day Smith was using her dad's "saws-all" tool to cut down some tree limbs in the backyard. When she was finished, she got the distinct impression of awe, and the phrase, "that was fast," floated through her mind. But it wasn't her thought. She already knew the saws-all was fast. She figures it was a thought sent her way from the resident handyman.

Another time, Smith pulled up some old, dirty carpet to check what was underneath. "I got the impression that I was supposed to use a sander and refinish the floor," she said. When she did, the wood floor looked magnificent.

Although she lived with a ghost for a couple of years, she said she "never sensed any fear. It was kind of cool having someone around who was interested in what I was doing."

Smith believes that it's to people's advantage to tune in to get help from the other side. "We ought to open ourselves up and perceive that kind of help. There are angels and close friends out there, people who really want to help us."

One day Smith served as an election judge and spent most of the day sitting next to an older woman. As time went on, they talked and became comfortable with one another. "I was telling her about this guy, and I described him to her and she said, 'That's Velton Mortenson.' He was one of the Mortenson family who lived there. His daughter owns the house now."

Smith found it difficult to move away. "The home just really loved us," she said. "It was the hardest thing to leave the love we felt in that house. It's like a woman who hadn't had any new stuff for years. She was finally getting a manicure and a new dress and new shoes. When we were moving out, it was hard to leave her."

Burial Ground

Dealing with burial grounds is a serious matter.

After she graduated from Brigham Young University in 1975, Anne McReynolds got a job as a social worker in Alberta, Canada. She moved with her daughters into a modest two-year-old house on a cul-de-sac.

"I remember that my daughters Kim and Jo slept in the one big bedroom with me," Anne said. "Darcy slept on the level just below ours in a family room, and Tammy chose a bedroom in the basement level beneath that one."

After spending about a week in their new house, the family was gathered together one evening when thirteen-year-old Tammy announced that she didn't want to go to bed. She told her family that every night, it sounded like people were throwing boxes up against the wall in the room adjoining hers. Even taking the family cat, Sammy, downstairs with her for comfort didn't help because Sammy simply growled at the noisy wall and ran off.

Tammy wasn't the only one who had noticed strange things happening.

"I could hear the living room was full of people talking and shuffling around all through the night," Darcy said. "I'd hear whispering, and when I was alone downstairs, I could just be almost asleep or just coming awake and there would be these voices talking right in my face. They sounded like little kids." Darcy demonstrated the talk, a disjointed tattoo of vowels and consonants delivered in a harsh, startling whisper.

"And I felt bound every time," she added. "About once each week, I felt as though I couldn't move when they were talking to me. Even after I moved upstairs, I could hear all these people every night."

Then Anne spoke up. "I tested my bedroom door. I opened it to a different place every night, just to see if the door moved, because I knew something was happening. In the morning, the door was always moved to a different position."

"We all said we didn't want to go to bed," Darcy remembered, who was twenty-one at the time. "We were all really scared. We finally decided that we'd just all sleep together in the living room."

By then, it was about 10 at night, and the mother and daughters were startled by a knock on their front door. At first they were hesitant to answer it, not sure who would be on the other side at that late hour. But finally they opened up to find two young men from their church standing there.

"Hello," Mr. Wright said, then seemed to be at a momentary loss for words. "Um…do you need us for anything?"

Anne looked at Darcy, who stared at her mother in astonishment. Then Anne turned back to the young men. "What made you come here?"

Mr. Wright shrugged. "We just had a feeling that we should come to this house. But if you don't need anything…"

"No, wait," Anne said. "Come in. Will you please bless this house and cast out the spirits?" She and her daughters explained what had been happening. After they'd told them everything, they all knelt in a circle and one of the men said a prayer, asking for the spirits that were there to leave, and blessing the family to live in peace.

As soon as Mr. Wright said "amen," the family was startled by three loud, heavy knocks sounding from the hallway. "It was like they were mad because they had to leave," said Darcy.

The young men rose to their feet and headed for the door.

"I was afraid to have them go," Anne said, "but they said it wouldn't be right for them to stay. When I told them I was scared to be alone with my girls, the other one, Mr. Kilpack, left his rubber overshoes just inside the front door. 'Maybe these will help give you some peace,' he told us."

"The spirits didn't bother us after that, and we soon moved away," Anne said. "But not before returning Mr. Kilpack's overshoes."

"We didn't stay there very long," Darcy agreed.

"Later we investigated the town records and found out that the subdivision was built on an old Indian burial ground," Anne said. "In that part of Alberta, it was probably the Blackfoot tribe's."

"There are lots of stories about respecting Indian burial graves," Darcy added. "The spirits weren't doing anything evil to us; they were just mischievous and trying to scare us off. Whoever built there desecrated their graves. They had no right to do that."

Lady on the Stairs

This ghost is determined to keep those around her safe.

Teri Morris and her husband, Glenn, own the Pherson House Bed and Breakfast on Main Street in Ephraim, Utah. Seven miles to the south is the town of Manti, where an annual summer outdoor production, *The Mormon Miracle Pageant*, is attended by thousands of people, creating an annual tourist boom. Teri and Glenn had only been open for nine months when the pageant season hit in 2004, filling their rooms to capacity each night of the performance.

After the whirlwind of activity, Teri felt like she could finally relax, since all the guests were gone.

She was mistaken.

"It was quite a change having the house so quiet after being so busy with the pageant," Teri said. "My husband, Glenn, and I were sitting in the back room when I heard somebody coming down the steps from upstairs. I said, 'I thought everybody left.'

"Glenn said, 'Maybe you'd better see what's going on.'

"It was dusk so you could just barely see without the lights. When I reached the front of the house, I noticed the image of a woman coming down the stairs. It was kind of like I could see through her, but she was really there. It was like a sheer material that you could look through. Her hair was pulled up in a bun and she wore old-fashioned clothes. I couldn't see the expression on her face, but I felt like we had a good rapport, that everything was all right. I also felt this cold feeling come over me, almost like I was frozen.

"As I stared at her, she soon dissipated. I asked myself if I had really seen what I thought I saw. When I turned around and walked in to where my husband was, he said, 'What's wrong with you? You look like you've seen a ghost.'

"I said, 'You won't believe me.'

"I had him touch me and he said, 'Oh, you're really cold!' I felt like I was made of ice."

Several things have happened since then. "She likes to play tricks," Teri said of the ghost. Keys turn up missing. Lights in empty rooms turn on, even though Teri and Glenn turn them off whenever they leave a room.

"One day we came in and I turned on the switch to the kitchen and the light didn't come on. We checked the fuses and even took the light apart but couldn't find a problem. Glenn said, 'It's like there's a dead circuit somewhere, or like there's another light switch that isn't working.'

"That's when I remembered that the breadboard was sitting in front of the only other light switch in the kitchen. We never used that one. When I checked, the switch had been moved to a center position so that it wouldn't make contact." They hadn't had any guests in the house, and all the doors had been locked while they were away.

It seems that the ghost also has an interest in guarding the house.

"There was a girl who wanted to stay overnight with us, but she didn't have quite enough money," Teri said. "She sat down to use the phone to try to call someone for more money. I wondered if I should just let her stay for the amount she could afford to pay.

"I had a decorative straw doll hanging on a nearby doorknob. Suddenly, the doll lifted off the knob and flew at the girl, landing on the floor before it reached her. The girl asked what made it do that. I said I didn't know."

Teri went to get something to clean up the straw that had spilled on the floor where the doll landed. "As I got the broom and dustpan, they flew out of my hands," Teri said. "I felt that this was an omen, so I told the girl I'd give her a ride to Manti where there were some motels that were within her price range. When I went to get my coat, the coat flew off the wall at me. Later I found out that the girl had been an accomplice in a recent bank robbery."

Teri's pretty sure that she's not the only one who's encountered their unusual houseguest.

"I've had people get up in the middle of the night and leave without saying anything," she said. "Stuff happens all over the house. You feel more of it upstairs than downstairs.

"One guy came to stay as the only guest upstairs. He came back down at ten PM and he said he had been called back to Salt Lake City and that he had to go right now.

"I had one young couple who got up early one morning and said, 'Don't worry about breakfast.' They were supposed to stay one more night, but they said, 'Keep the money, we're leaving.' It's happened with two couples and one man so far."

And it's only happened since Teri saw the ghost on the stairs.

Teri thinks that the ghost may be a former occupant of the house. She even asked the elderly son of a lady who used to live there about it. "I asked, 'Was the house haunted when you lived here?' He said 'no.' He was kind of taken aback. I didn't tell him that I suspected it was his mother; I just told him that I thought we had a ghost.

"Karen, the previous owner, said that she wouldn't stay in the house alone. It's too big and lonely. After I saw the ghost, I asked her if it was haunted. She just smiled."

Teri's affinity to sense spirits may stem from an experience she had as a young woman. "I was going about forty miles per hour down a side street and a mosquito flew in the window," she said. "When I swatted at the mosquito, I must have turned the wheel because I ran into a parked car. The next thing I remember is being up above the car. I felt disconnected and at total peace. There's a whole different feeling out of your body, a total feeling of... I don't know if it's love. We know what love is because of what we can give to each other, but love isn't really an adequate word for it. There's really nothing to explain what you feel.

"Then I saw this lady run out of her house. She pulled my car door open and said, 'Oh no, she's dead!'

"Another lady ran up and said, 'I called the ambulance.'

"I had been wearing a wig, and I could see that it had flown off my head and landed in the back seat of the car. Then I heard the sirens and looked down the street to see the ambulance coming. Then I felt pure pain as I was sucked back into my body. I was trying to get air in my lungs and trying to breathe. Then I got out of the car, and they all stood back. They cancelled the ambulance because I was walking around, but when I got to the back of the car, I collapsed again. The ambulance turned around and came back.

"A few times I faded out and I kept coming back. When I got to the hospital, they gave me a fifty-fifty chance. I was in intensive care for a week and a half and in recovery for another week and a half.

"Maybe that's the reason I was able to see the ghost," Teri said. "Glenn could see other things that happened. He's felt the cold where she was. If you go to the spot where I saw her, it's very cold, like an air conditioner."

Teri doesn't mind having a ghost staying at her bed and breakfast, especially one that looks out for undesirable houseguests. "I think it's kind of neat," Teri says.

Anyone who'd like to spend a night can perhaps find out for themselves.

The Old Rock House

These ghosts played favorites.

It was 1991 when Liz Snow's friend, Veronica, said that she knew the perfect place for Liz to buy. Liz went along to see the old rock house half-hidden behind an ancient apricot tree. She thought it was the saddest thing she'd ever seen. The "For Sale" sign pasted in the window was off-kilter, like a droopy eyelid. "It looked desolate," Liz remembered.

Still, she got out of the car and followed her friend over the little ditch that ran in front of the property and across the patches of weeds to take a closer look. They rubbed a clear spot on one of the house's grimy windows and peered inside while Veronica's son, Pete, wandered around a corner of the house.

The sight that greeted their eyes was even worse than Liz had imagined. A lumpy water heater stood guard in a suit of rusty armor over the litter scattered across the floor. The walls were peeling in uneven strips of diseased wallpaper. Where the kitchen sink should have been was a big lump of something that was hard to identify in the dim interior.

Pete came running back around the side of the house at full speed, nearly bumping into his mother.

"Peter, watch out!" Veronica reprimanded him.

"You guys, the door on the back is open," he said, breathless with the news.

Veronica looked at Liz with shining eyes. "Isn't this awesome? Now we can go in and look around!"

"Uh, isn't that called trespassing?" Liz asked.

"But the door's unlocked," Veronica said. "It's for sale. How can they sell it if nobody looks inside?"

It took some coaxing, but Veronica finally got Liz into the little house.

"The sink was tipped sideways and set into a hole in the kitchen counter," Liz said. "There were no faucets." The walls were streaked with soot and the floor was riddled with mouse droppings.

Veronica grabbed Liz's arm and said with ill-concealed excitement, "Every time I drive down this road and see this house, I get the feeling, *this is Liz's house*. Every single time! You've got to write down the phone number."

"Obviously, Veronica was looking at possibilities while I was looking at desolation," Liz said.

Liz couldn't deny that she'd always had a dream in the back of her mind to live in a quaint cottage in a small town, with roses growing wild under the windows and a stream gurgling through the property.

But an irrigation ditch wasn't exactly a stream, and this droopy, one-story bungalow wasn't what she'd been dreaming of.

With Veronica's coaxing, Liz got her husband, Gabriel, to look over the place. The original rock structure consisted of two fair sized rooms with a large, arched doorway between them. A smaller room was walled off on the east end with a single door in the center. Sometime in the house's history, a wooden addition had been built onto the south side to accommodate a kitchen, bathroom, and one small bedroom.

Without much enthusiasm, Liz and Gabriel took some pictures, wrote down the phone number, and headed back home to southern California.

"When we got back, we found out that the house we'd

been renting had been put up for sale, and we had to find another place to live," Liz said.

The miles between her and the little old house had softened her memory. She decided to call and find out more about it.

"When the owner of the house said she only wanted $8,000 for it, I thought that surely we could come up with that much," Liz said.

Ironically, Gabriel was then employed by a moving company, who agreed to move the couple's possessions free of charge.

When Liz and Gabriel arrived, at last, at what they thought was their fairy tale house, instead they found a wolf in the bed. There was no furnace, no central heating system of any kind. They had to rely on a single wood stove to keep them warm in the winter.

But Liz got used to it. "I always felt a feeling of comfort and belonging, even though there were plenty of challenges to living in an old house. The pipes froze often in the winter, the primitive electrical fuses were blowing out all the time, and it was challenging. But it never felt scary."

Liz set about making her little house into a comfortable home. She re-papered the walls, scrubbed the floors, and hung pretty towels in the bathroom. She hung pictures and carried fresh flowers indoors during the summer to brighten up the house.

Liz said that she often experienced feelings of love and peace from her family members who've passed on while she lived in the house. "I think that the lady the house was originally built for hangs around in there too," Liz said. "My friend, Lois, came in once and said, 'Oooo, you have company!' She was referring to the spirits that she felt inside my house."

Four years later, Liz and Gabriel welcomed a baby girl, Michelle, into their home. With the addition of a new little family member, the house seemed to shrink. Also, the responsibility of chopping wood in the winter seemed to loom like a dark specter when they had an infant to consider.

Since their house was paid off by this time, the family decided to build a new house, complete with a furnace, on the same half-acre lot.

The city told them that in order to build, they'd have to remove the old house. Just in time, the house made it onto the historic register. "We had to tear down the addition," Liz said, "but we were able to keep the original 1874 structure.

"When we demolished the kitchen, there was a header above the kitchen window, and there were rocks above that. In the gap between the header and the rock wall, I found a bundle of old sagebrush tied with twine. Someone told me that people used to use sage in order to bless their house in the olden days," Liz said.

The attic in the addition had been insulated with autumn leaves, blackened with age. When they tore up the kitchen floor, Liz found an intricate silver spoon, worn and tarnished black. Liz polished the spoon and now uses it in her sugar bowl, a gift from the old house.

Even with a new home, Liz visited the old house often. "We used it for quilting in summer and storage when friends and family were moving and needed a place to keep their belongings." The bungalow was used as storage for five different families.

"When my sister, Jean, came during a transition period in her life, I offered to set up her furniture in the old house so she could have her own private space if she wanted it," Liz said. "So we moved her stuff in. I set it up, decorated it with her own quilts, and tried to make it cheery. After she saw it, she decided she wanted to sleep there instead of in our new house."

Jean was Liz's favorite sister when they were children, yet somewhere along their separate life paths, Jean had become opinionated, harsh, and judgmental. "She made me cry while I was setting her things up in the old rock house,"

Liz said. "I tried to hide it, but when she went over to the new house for a minute, I didn't hold back."

That night, Jean slept in the old house. The next morning, she walked across the lawn to where Liz was fixing breakfast. "She came in looking shell-shocked," Liz remembered.

"Your ghosts have been scratching me all night," Jean complained. "They're mean. Will you have a talk with them?"

Ghosts? Liz was shocked. The feeling in her old house had always been peaceful. "You must have brought them with you," Liz said.

Jean didn't agree, and asked Gabriel to get the ghosts out of the old house.

Gabriel trudged across the lawn and entered the bungalow. "I told the ghosts that it was very temporary, and to please be patient with Jean and quit bugging her," Gabriel said.

"It didn't work," Liz said. "Jean tried to sleep out there every night, even though I told her she could sleep in the house."

Jean continued to criticize and make hurtful comments. "She made me cry every day, so the ghosts would make her cry at night," Liz said.

Not only was Jean afflicted with scratching ghosts, she also had an earwig invasion.

"She kept a humidifier running all the time," Liz remembered. "The earwigs really liked it. She was going to stay all summer, but after two weeks she couldn't take it any longer and moved out."

After a moment of thought, Liz said, "I guess it depends on what kind of person you are, what you bring with you, and what you attract. I thought I was offering her paradise and she thought it was hell."

The Grim Reaper

The canyon has a history of bloody massacres, and this ghost isn't about to let passersby forget it.

Doug and his wife, Merilee, left Provo, Utah at about 11 PM in 1993. They had their seven-year-old grandson, Trent, with them.

"We'd purchased some lumber so I could build my mom a deck," Doug explained. "I was pulling the trailer with an SUV and the trailer was totally loaded with lumber." Doug paused, then added with a wry laugh, "I probably had it overloaded." He admitted that he'd gotten all the lumber he needed for the deck in one trip because he didn't want to have to go back to the city again.

"We stopped to get a little something to eat in Nephi. By then, it was getting close to midnight."

Doug remembers that it started raining about the time they headed up Salt Creek Canyon east of Nephi. "It was raining really hard," Doug said. "It was raining so hard that I had my wipers on full blast and it was barely keeping it clear. I was doing twenty miles an hour, tops."

Partway into Salt Creek Canyon is a little dam where motorists can often spot fishermen, but not at midnight in a downpour. As they passed the popular fishing spot, Doug had no clue what was waiting for them on the road up ahead.

"Probably about half a mile past the dam, you go in a slight dip and there's a little pool there. By then I bet I was going less than ten miles an hour with this load of lumber. I had the car in low gear. When we started up the little rise on the other side of the dip, we could see that there was something in the middle of the road."

With the heavy rain, it was hard to make out exactly what was waiting for them. It was natural to assume that a deer was standing there, watching them inch up the incline, but what was the light colored line that vertically bisected the thing? "It seemed like it was almost a yellow colored staff, but I wonder if the light from the car hit it, and with the rain, made it kind of glare. It was very noticeable, and it was as tall as the thing in the road," Doug said.

Trying to pull the heavy load up the incline on a slick road forced the overloaded SUV down to five miles per hour. As they drew steadily closer, the thing in the road took on the shape of a person. "When we got really close, it was this thing dressed in a really long black cloak and it had a hood over so you couldn't see its face," Doug said. "It was like the Grim Reaper. I thought to myself, 'That's really tall.'"

Merilee was in the backseat, leaning forward so that her head was between Doug and Trent. As they drew abreast of the thing, it shook its staff in their direction.

"It was taller than our vehicle, so it had to have been way over six feet," Doug said. "It was facing us and we think it was looking at us. All you could see was the hood."

They passed the thing so close that Doug said the cloak could easily have brushed the side of the car. "It was very strange," Doug said. He also mentioned that he couldn't see any hands, because they were hidden inside the cloak.

Once it was behind them, there was a moment of shocked silence. Then Merilee said, "Did you see what I saw?"

"Yeah," Doug said.

"It wasn't standing on the road," Trent said.

His grandparents looked at him in surprise. "He told us that he'd seen some space between it and the pavement," Doug said.

"I hope it didn't jump on our trailer," Merilee whispered, casting a nervous glance out the back window. But all she saw was a wall of water cascading down the glass.

They got home in a drizzle of rain without encountering any other unexplained beings along the way.

The next day, Doug couldn't help but mention the strange incident to his coworkers. One suggested that it might have been kids out playing a prank. Another said that it could have been a bored sheepherder.

But another coworker had a different opinion.

"Someone told me there had been stories of strange things happening to other people traveling Salt Creek Canyon. I really don't know what it was," Doug said. "But who would be standing in the middle of the road past midnight in a downpour playing games? It was a very strange thing. And it didn't look drenched. The cloak was not sticking to the body, it was hanging loose. If you'd seen something off the road or in the distance, you might wonder about what you saw, but this thing was so close, there was no question."

No One There

Is what Pepper sees real? Or is she just dreaming?

"I don't know if what I see are ghosts or not," Pepper said with a shrug. "I usually only see them when I wake up in the early morning while it's still dark."

It started when Pepper moved with her family from the eastern United States to a small western town in the 1970s. "The first time it happened, I was about twelve. I slept on the top bunk while my big sister slept in the bottom bunk," Pepper said.

"One morning I woke up really early in the bedroom of this century-old Victorian home we rented. It was maybe three or four in the morning. I was kind of surprised to see this blond boy about my age sitting on the edge of the twin bed in our room that nobody was using, talking to himself and gesturing with his hands. I couldn't hear what he said, though." Pepper gave a little laugh. "I didn't even feel scared. I pretty much wondered if I looked all right! I mean, I didn't want any boy, ghost or not, to see me with serious bed head."

Pepper sat up and ran a hand over her hair. The boy didn't look up.

"Hello," Pepper said.

The boy still didn't react, seeming to be absorbed in his own silent monologue.

"Then he just faded away," Pepper said. "I stared at the empty bed for a minute, wondering if I'd really seen someone there or not. Then I lay back down and closed my eyes. I peeked a couple of times just to check if he'd come back, but he didn't."

By the time Pepper was a teenager, the family had moved to another house on the edge of town. Beyond their house stretched fields and mountains. Again, the house was an old one, the original structure having been built of adobe at least a hundred years earlier, then added onto by subsequent owners.

"There was a bathroom window in the wall next to the tub," Pepper said. "It was really too big for a bathroom window. Even though it was frosted, you could kind of see through it." The window faced a carport at the back of the house.

One evening, Pepper was showering when she saw a blurred face at the bathroom window. "I screamed and ducked," Pepper said. "It looked like it was a man with a red knitted hat on."

Pepper slithered over the side of the tub. Before she could even get wrapped in a towel, her older brother, Ron, was pounding on the door asking if she was all right.

"I told him I saw someone looking in the window," Pepper said.

Ron took off and hit the door running. After a search of the carport, he came back to say that he hadn't seen anyone coming or going.

After that, the family got a curtain for the bathroom window.

Those incidents were the furthest things from Pepper's mind by the time she got married in the spring of 1978. "That summer we went camping in a spot on the back side of Mount Timpanogas," Pepper remembered. "We were sleeping in a two-man tent, which was just the right size for us."

Somewhere in the early morning hours when the stars were still out, Pepper woke up and looked out the tent flap. She was astonished to see a toddler of about two or three years old moving around in the sagebrush.

"There was a piece of sagebrush between me and the child," Pepper said. "But I could distinctly see that he was wearing a blue and red coat with a hood. The child was facing away from me, but I got the feeling it was a little boy."

Pepper woke her husband, Craig, with an urgent shake. "There's a little boy out there," she said, pointing out through the tent flap.

Craig squinted into the moon-washed landscape. "There's no one there," he answered.

Pepper couldn't believe her ears. "He's right there," she said, pointing to the toddler that she could see moving around in the brush about fifteen yards away.

"Where?" Craig asked, narrowing his eyes in the direction Pepper was pointing.

"Right there in the bushes," Pepper said. "He's wearing a red and blue coat. Can't you see him?"

After a moment of scanning the bushes, Craig said, "There's no one there."

"Yes, he is!" Pepper insisted, staring at the little figure so hard that she had to blink. When she blinked, it felt as if there was a shift in the atmosphere. The little person seemed to be only half there, and an instant later, was gone. There was no longer a toddler in a red and blue coat needing to be rescued.

The next time Pepper saw someone was after she and Craig had three children. "We were in a split entry rental house in Salt Lake City," Pepper said. "I was sleeping one night when, for no apparent reason, I woke up in the early morning and opened my eyes. Leaning with his back against the bedroom wall was a dark haired man in his early 30s with stubble on his chin. He was kind of good-looking, except for the fact that he had his head lowered and was staring out at me from underneath angry eyebrows. His arms were folded across his chest and I got the distinct impression that he didn't want us there."

Pepper didn't wait for the man to fade. She closed her eyes, pressed herself against her sleeping husband's back, and pulled the covers over her head.

"We only lived in that house for about three months," Pepper said. "One of my sons had some pretty bad nightmares while sleeping downstairs with his brothers in that house."

The last experience Pepper had wasn't from seeing anything, but came from a feeling. "We'd just had our fourth child," Pepper said. "We were living in a rural town, and Craig had gone to his night job. I was home with the older children asleep in their bedroom, and the baby woke up around 11:30 PM or maybe midnight. I was sitting in a rocking chair in the living room, taking care of the baby, when I felt this unreasonable sense of fear creep over me. I looked around but couldn't see or hear anything. The feeling gradually grew stronger and stronger until I felt like I was cemented in position in my chair. I was terrified. I don't remember feeling so scared in my life. I didn't even want the baby to move, and I nearly broke a sweat for fear my chair would rock. I'm not even sure why I didn't want anything to move. It was like I might attract attention from whatever invisible thing was scaring me so badly."

After sitting there, frozen with fear for a minute or two, Pepper decided that she had to do something to break free. What if one of her children needed her? What if one of them wandered out looking for her?

"I began to think in my mind, 'Heavenly Father, please help me, Heavenly Father, please help me,'" Pepper said. "I thought it over and over until at last I was speaking it out loud. It felt as if the fear slipped off of me and flowed across the floor and out. At last I could move, and I got up and went to check on my children. They were all peacefully asleep.

"I took the baby into bed with me, and with tears running down my face, I thanked Father in Heaven for helping me."

Pepper never figured out what it was that had created such erratic fear on that dark night.

"Hey, I don't know exactly what it is I've seen," Pepper said. "Maybe they're just leftover pieces of dreams superimposed on my waking environment." Of the man in the shower window, she says, "I don't know, maybe that was just a reflection of something. Maybe it was me! It wasn't really clear, you know. I just thought it was a man's face, but I could have been wrong."

Woman in the Chair

Hell hath no fury like a forgotten woman.

Everyone was talking about it. It was the most morbid incident that had happened in the small town since the pioneer and Indian fights of the wild west. It was even more bizarre than old Mrs. Sutton lying on her kitchen floor for a day and a half after she'd suffered a stroke. She was finally discovered by the mailman, who called for help and saved her life.

No one saved Mrs. Bits. In fact, Mr. Bits left his wife sitting in a living room chair for three days after she died. When questioned, he claimed that he didn't know she was dead.

It wasn't any secret that Mr. and Mrs. Bits didn't get along anymore. They hadn't for some time. But like ants marching from their anthill, not looking left or right, the Bits kept on living in the same house, doing the same things they'd done for so long that they couldn't remember any other way. Their once loving relationship from nearly fifty years earlier had turned into automation, going through the motions of living without really caring about each other. They didn't like one another, but what were they to do? Neither one had anywhere else to go, so they just stayed in the same house, living as two strangers under the same roof.

Even though he was retired, Mr. Bits had a habit of getting up every morning and fixing his own breakfast, then leaving the house for most of the day. When he came home in the evening, he'd have supper alone and go to bed. What did he care if Mrs. Bits sat in a stuffed chair in the living room? He didn't have anything to say to her, and he didn't care whether she went to bed or slept in the chair.

Mrs. Bits' true condition was discovered when their grown daughter came to visit. The authorities were called, there was a funeral and lots of gossip, then as time went on the gossip wore thin as new events cropped up for the townspeople to talk about. The bizarre incident was pushed further back into the town's history.

Later on, Mr. Bits died. After his children cleared all the mementos they wanted from the small two-story house, they put it up for sale. For a long time there were no takers.

At last, Eliza Quirk decided to buy the house. It was going cheap, and she planned to use it as a rental. Since the family had only taken what they wanted and left the rest, cleanup was a big job. Quirk had to wade through all the things that the Bits had accumulated over the years.

At last the little house was clean, painted, and ready to rent. The first family moved in and seemed satisfied, but after a short time they moved out. It didn't take Quirk long to find another family who wanted to rent the charming little home, but they also moved after a short time. The third family that rented the home only stayed a little while too, but this time they told Quirk that someone else was in the house.

"They said they weren't afraid of her because she didn't do anything to frighten them," Quirk said. But still, it seemed that Quirk had to do something about the ghost, because it wasn't doing her any good to have an empty rental house.

In talking about the situation with others, Mrs. Quirk met a lady named Magda who had experience working with ghosts and sending them to the light. "I asked if she would help," Quirk said. "I also told two men from church what the situation was, and they came with us too."

Once they were inside the house, the four of them had a prayer before Magda started talking to the ghost, coaxing it to communicate with her.

After a few minutes, she turned to the others and told them that the ghost was Mrs. Bits, but she didn't want to talk because she was very angry.

Magda didn't give up. She kept entreating the ghost to tell her what was wrong. Finally, Mrs. Bits told Magda that she was upset because her husband hadn't even noticed when she'd died. "How could he not know?" she demanded. It seemed that her intense hurt and anger kept her pinned to the spot where the offense had occurred. Once she was heard, however, the ghost confessed to Magda, "I don't know what to do now."

"For about half an hour, Magda asked Mrs. Bits if she would like to rest and be happy, and Mrs. Bits indicated that she would like that very much," said Quirk. "So Magda told her to look for the light and go toward it. After several minutes, Magda told us that Mrs. Bits had left."

There have been no more complaints from renters or unexpected vacancies since then.

Haunted Cradle

This ghost fled from an encounter with a ouija board.

Janice Ray had a penchant for antiques, so she was delighted with the old baby furniture she found while vacationing in Texas. After returning to Las Vegas, her husband, Paul, carried the old cradle, high chair, and wooden potty chair into their house.

It didn't take long for the Rays to realize that they'd brought home more than antiques. "Right when we came home, we heard running upstairs, but everyone was downstairs. It was a lot of noise, like someone running really hard," Ray said.

Janice asked Paul to put the cradle in a corner of her son's room on the second floor. She set the high chair up in the foyer with a plant in it, and the potty chair held a plant in the downstairs bathroom.

"One night Paul and I were sitting in the family room, which is just beneath our son's room," Janice said. "All of a sudden it sounded like a huge elephant walking across the floor overhead. It went through the middle of the room and out where the fireplace is. With a bed in the middle of the bedroom, there was no place for anyone to stomp across the floor. There was no one home but me and Paul."

Several months later, the heavy wooden fireplace mantel fell off the wall and crashed into the hearthstones. "It just fell right off," Janice said. "It was the same wall that sounded like an elephant went through it."

Janice believed that the strange occurrences stemmed from the antiques, especially the cradle, because nothing like that had ever happened before.

"Most of the things happened upstairs," Janice said. "It was mostly in my daughter's room, sometimes in the foyer, and then in the attic."

One strange incident involved a pair of ceramic chickens that decorated the top of Janice's microwave oven. After the antique baby furniture arrived, Janice would find the chickens turned around facing the wall. "I was accusing Paul all the time, because I was just sure he was doing it, but then it happened when he wasn't home," Janice said.

All of the bedrooms in the house were upstairs. The Ray's teenage daughter, Brenda, had a bedroom that included a door into the attic. "We didn't want her to be get scared, so we didn't mention anything about the ghost to her," Janice said. "My daughter gets real scared being alone; she's still that way now and she's thirty-four years old. That's why we were so careful not to say anything."

The attic was narrow and ran the whole length of the house. Brenda often said she heard noises up there, as if someone were playing in the attic. "There was a band rehearsing music that we could hear from a block or so away, and we'd just say it must be the band," Janice said.

But Brenda's parents couldn't blame the band for the malfunctioning lights.

"The light switches in that house were the kind that you dial, so when we turned them they'd gradually go from dim to bright. But then, of their own accord, the lights started coming on full brightness, then they'd just go off. To go from off to on with no dimming in between was really strange. But that's what happened," Janice said.

Brenda didn't seem surprised when her mother talked to her about the lights. "That happens all the time," Brenda said.

Next, the ceiling fan started acting up. "We had a fan in the family room and it would just come on," Janice said. "You'd think it was just an electrical short, but it wasn't. It always happened when you were having a conversation with somebody."

Paul and Janice couldn't keep the strange events from Brenda indefinitely, especially not when one of her friends told her she had a ghost.

"She was a senior in high school," Janice said. "One of her friends named Brandy walked into the house, turned to Brenda and said, 'You have a spirit, don't you?'

"Brenda said, 'How do you know?'

"Brandy said, 'Because I have a spirit too.'"

Brandy said that her spirit would jump on her bed, and she could see the shape of its footprints press into the bed covers every time it bounced down. It would manipulate physical objects, turning pictures and other things around all the time. It was a mischievous spirit, and when Brandy's family moved, it moved right along with them.

After this conversation, Brenda would often bring a blanket downstairs with her and settle onto the couch. If Janice asked her why she wasn't sleeping in her room, she'd say, "There's a tea party going on upstairs and I don't want to be there."

Then the baby started crying.

"It was the first time we knew the ghost was a baby," Janice said. "Never in my entire life will I forget that baby crying beside my bed. It was pitiful."

The first time it happened, Janice and Paul were asleep. "It was probably about the crack of daylight because it was still mostly dark but just barely light in the room," Janice remembered. "We could hear this baby cry, and my husband thought it was one of the grandkids who spent the night. But it wasn't. Paul was just lying there, not doing anything about it because he's a man. I finally got conscious enough that I sat up and asked, 'What's that?' It stopped instantly.

But it was right by my side of the bed."

The Rays lived in that home from 1980 to 1995. It was after they brought the antiques home in 1981 when Janice first heard the baby cry. Over the ensuing years, she heard it about fifteen times, and it was always upstairs.

"There were many, many times when we were alone and things were going on upstairs," Janice said. "This may seem strange, but I never once went up to check, because like the baby by my bed, when you sat up and said something, it went away."

Sometimes Janice heard the baby cry in her daughter's bedroom. "Brenda would be in the bathroom and we could hear the baby crying, and we could tell that it was coming from her room. When I got to the doorway it would stop. It happened to enough people that it wasn't like it was just me hearing it.

"Our son, Ralph, was away from home when we moved into the house. When he heard about the ghost later, he pooh-poohed the whole thing. He didn't believe in it at all."

But when he came back home, he began to wonder.

"He'd be getting ready to go on patrol as a policeman, and he'd hear someone out in the hall. Thinking he was alone, he'd call, 'Mom?' but no one answered, so he'd yank open the door, but no one was there. It didn't take long for him to be a believer."

Sometimes the attic door in Brenda's room would be open, then would shut of its own accord.

"Paul's brother, Hilary, came from Texas. He thought we were putting him on. The lights would go off and on, and he'd try to stop it, but they wouldn't stop," Janice said. "We had people want to come and stay in our house overnight after they heard about all the things that were going on."

One summer evening, the Rays had unexpected visitors. "My daughter's boyfriend, Wade, and his friend, Spence, were throwing pebbles at Brenda's window, but they couldn't get her attention."

Eventually, the two boys decided to circle the house and see if they could come up with another subtle way to let Brenda know they were there. "As they were walking around the garage, Spence was in front and Wade was following him. Something took hold of Wade and threw him against the garage door. He knew it wasn't Spence, because he could see him in front, but there was no one behind him."

On another occasion, Wade was sitting on the couch in the living room, waiting along with the Rays' dog, Kristi, for Brenda to return from getting something out of the garage. When Wade heard footsteps, he naturally assumed that Brenda was coming back. To his astonishment, the footsteps moved across the floor and up the stairs, but he couldn't see anyone. If he doubted his sanity about what he was hearing, Kristi verified it. "The dog was watching it go up the stairs too," Janice said.

One day, Janice's nephews, Jason and Jerald, came to visit while the Rays were gone. Not knowing the house was empty, the boys rang the bell and waited. The lights went on upstairs. They heard something moving at the top of the stairs, then the sound of footsteps come down the staircase. Whatever was inside the house moved to the opposite side of the door and stood there. The boys even saw its shadow, but the door didn't open.

The hair rose on the back of Jason's neck. Something wasn't right. He and Jerald hurried away, certain that what had come to the door was not their aunt or uncle or either of their cousins.

They'd heard the ghost stories. One time, after questioning Brenda about the noises she heard in the attic, they'd brought some friends over and challenged them to walk the length of the haunted attic for a reward of five dollars each. Their friends moved up the staircase, cautiously surveying the room. They made their careful way along the wooden floor, quiet except for their echoing footsteps. They reached the end and started back. Darting looks from side to side, they returned to the top of the stairs and collected their money. Nothing spooky happened.

Now, with the ghost at the door, Jason and Jerald decided to try and figure out what was really going on.

"They came back with a couple of friends and a ouija board," Janice said. "They wanted to use it to find out what the spirit in our house was."

The boys went into the backyard and set some lawn chairs in a circle on the patio. As soon as they sat down, they could feel something come into their circle. It wasn't something they could see, but it was definitely there.

All of a sudden, the pointer on the ouija board spun around and shot straight up into the air. The boys were so startled that they threw the ouija board and took off running. The splash of the board landing in the swimming pool made Jerald turn back just long enough to see it sliding into the water.

The boys went back to Jason and Jerald's house and grabbed a Bible. Then the four of them headed back to the Rays'. Sticking close together, they made their way around the house. When they approached the circle of chairs, what they saw made their skin crawl. "The ouija board was sitting right there in the center of the circle of chairs, the pointer exactly in place," Janice said.

Since the boys all knew the ouija board had landed in the pool, they couldn't imagine who, or what, had put it back and set it up, ready to use. But none of them wanted to have anything more to do with it. They turned and ran.

"When we came home, we saw the circle of chairs and knew we hadn't left them that way. Jason and Jerald came back with my brother-in-law, Jerry, and their two friends. They went upstairs to Brenda's room and went through the attic door. Whatever it was slammed the door on them while they were up there. The boys were so scared that they went running down the stairs, through the door, and out of the house."

The boys dove into their car and sped away without waiting for Jerry to catch up.

"My sister-in-law, Beverly, called from home to tell us that the kids were at a service station down the road. They were pretty upset, to the point that they were throwing up."

Jason and Jerald never set foot in the Rays' house again.

In April of 2005, Jerald told his Aunt Janice that he still has nightmares about that house and the events that took place there. "He's 35 or 36 years old," Janice said. "And he told me that a couple of days ago, he had another nightmare about being trapped in that house and not being able to get out."

After that night, all the ghostly activity stopped.

"I was really mad at them when I realized the spirit was gone, because I felt like it had a home with us," Janice said. "I don't know what they did to it, but they obviously did something. I told them, 'That wasn't nice of you to come over to our house and mess with our spirit.'

"We bought the antiques shortly after we moved into the house. The strange things happened over the course of months and months, it went on for nearly fifteen years. It was never anything we were afraid of. We knew it was a child and it didn't do mean things." After a moment of thought, Janice added, "I thought it was one ghost, but maybe there were more, because a baby couldn't throw that boy up against the garage. I never felt like it was two, but as a spirit, I guess maybe you have more power, enough to throw a boy against a door. Some things you just can't explain."

Lonely Little Boy

It's an odd feeling to hold a ghost on your lap.

Janice Ray has encountered spirits on more than one occasion.

"We visited the first courthouse in San Diego," she said. "It was the judge's home, and the courthouse was attached. People loved to come there in the olden days."

And it seems that guests from long ago still like to gather.

"There were always social events," Janice said. "You could smell gingerbread cooking. You could smell the judge's cigars. You could hear whispered conversations going on around you in the courtroom. They had pictures of apparitions that people had photographed in the place hanging on the walls."

Janice seems to have a particular affinity for children's ghosts. "Someone had a ghost living in the closet under her stairs," Janice said. "It was a friendly spirit, and it was okay until she had a baby. Then the ghost got jealous. It would put things in the baby's bed, and move the bed, so they had it exorcised."

Another ghost that Janice knows about firsthand lived for awhile with a friend of hers in Boulder City by Lake Mead. "My friend lived by the lake in a real nice brand new home, but it had a mean spirit. It would move all their furniture and block the door so they couldn't get in their house. It would block the bathroom door too. They had a little Buddha statue that they kept in their living room. Every time they came home, that statue was always turned to face the wall. Finally, her husband got fed up and yelled, 'Whoever that is, just leave my stuff alone!' A few seconds later, the glass shower door shattered into a million pieces, but there was no one in the bathroom. The only explanation they could come up with was that the ghost got mad, and it was as if it were saying, 'Don't tell me what to do! *Crash!*' It just wasn't something they wanted around."

Another lady Janice knows fell down her stairs, but before she hit the bottom, something grabbed hold of her and stopped her fall. It was something she couldn't see, but later on, she discovered the prints of fingers on her stomach, right where she'd been grabbed.

Around 1975, Janice made friends with Emma, a sixty-year-old wife of a career military man. They met when Emma moved into a house across the street from Janice. It took some time and repeated visits before Emma would talk much. "She kept to herself," Janice said. "She was a real introverted person."

Perhaps that was because the things she had to say would be hard for some people to believe.

Eventually, Emma told Janice about her dreams. "Emma would dream things and then they would happen, like an earthquake or tornado or some other event, and she could always tell when someone was going to die," Janice said. "One time, her mother appeared to her, and Emma asked, 'What are you doing here?' Her mother said, 'I just came to say good-bye.' The next day, Emma found out that her mother had died.

"She hated it. She didn't know what her gift was for, and she didn't know what to do with it. She'd had it for so many years, and it wasn't something she talked to very many people about."

Then Emma told Janice about Jimmy.

"The military wives would stick together when their husbands were gone," Janice said. "One time, when her husband was stationed in San Diego, California, Emma was at a party with the other wives. One of the ladies said she had a spirit with her. They'd ask the spirit a 'yes' or 'no' question, and it would tap the table leg to answer. One of the questions was whether anyone else in the room had a spirit too. The answer was that Emma did."

The ladies played with the spirits, asking them questions and getting the answers through taps until they determined that Emma's spirit was a seven year old red-headed boy with freckles named Jimmy, who had died from typhoid fever in 1850.

As Emma's children grew, they would play with Jimmy too. It didn't bother Emma to have him around, and her kids loved playing with him.

"He wasn't a bad spirit," Janice said. "There are lots of bad spirits, but I think there are good ones, too."

Emma told Janice that she used to talk to Jimmy a lot. It was a social thing they did when people came over. The spirit could even predict the winners of races.

"When they were in Arkansas, there were dog and horse races," Janice said. "Jimmy would tell them who was going to win, but if they bet on it, it wouldn't happen. It only came true if there was no money riding on it."

Then Emma's kids got married and moved away and she didn't pay attention to Jimmy for a long time.

"She told me she hadn't talked to him for awhile," Janice said. "Her husband was away at the time, and she said, 'Let's go see if Jimmy's still around. He's probably mad at me because I haven't talked to him for so long.'"

The two ladies set up a card table and sat on opposite sides. They placed their hands on top, palms flat against the surface, their fingers stretched toward each other.

Emma said, "I know you're mad at me, Jimmy, but you

aren't mad at Janice, so go get up onto her lap."

What happened next was undeniable and indescribable. "Something went right up my toes and into my body, and it felt really weird," Janice said. "I immediately started crying. I was sobbing, with big tears running down my face."

Janice was frightened by the strange sensation of having something she couldn't see taking up the same space she was in. The feeling was so unnerving, combined with her inexplicable tears, that she jumped up from her chair and said, "Okay, it's over, it's done, we're through."

Janice has no doubt that little Jimmy, whatever he is, definitely sat on her lap. She believes that he must have been upset and crying, because she was crying as soon as she felt him. "I don't know what would have happened if I had let it go on," Janice said. And she doesn't particularly want to know, either.

Shortly afterward, Emma moved away.

"It was certainly interesting," Janice said. "That's been thirty years ago. These things are really hard to explain."

The Face in the Window

The glass reflected a most unexpected sight.

Snowflakes smacked against the windshield of the vintage 1973 VW Bug as Dylan pulled it around the back of his family's house. Peering past the wipers that swept the tiny white flakes aside, Dylan could see the headlights illuminate his parking spot just beneath the large kitchen window. He stopped the engine and let himself out, his shoes crunching on ice so cold it crackled. He glanced at the dark window, wishing he could be inside where it was warm, but there was something he had to do first. "I plugged an extension cord to a light that I put just under the hood to make my car start better on cold mornings," Dylan said.

Once his task was complete, Dylan tiptoed into the kitchen, locked the door, and flipped on the light. He rubbed his hands together to get some feeling back into them before rummaging in the refrigerator for a bedtime snack. Food in hand, he headed for his room. "My bedroom was on the second floor, up a flight of stairs that creaked with every step," Dylan said. "It was quite a chore to work my way up the stairs without waking my dad."

The house was over a hundred years old, and although Dylan had asked his father more than once if they couldn't just replace the old floors, the answer was always that they were good enough as they were.

"It was around midnight when I got ready for bed," Dylan said. "I walked to a small window that looked down on our backyard to see if it had quit snowing." He was amazed to see that not only had the snow stopped, but the moon had come out, spreading soft light over a backyard as smooth and white as spilled milk.

When Dylan's eyes dropped to his VW, he groaned. The dark car window mirrored a square of warm yellow radiating from the kitchen. He'd forgotten to turn off the light.

Before he could turn around to go downstairs and switch it off, Dylan noticed a figure in the reflection. "In the middle of the window, looking out, I could see a man," Dylan said. "At first, I thought Dad was up and had turned on the light, and was standing there looking out at the new snowfall. But as I looked closer, I could see that this man had a long black beard and an old style top hat on. He was dressed in black clothing with what seemed to be a white shirt and a black bow-tie."

Shocked and dismayed, Dylan stepped back and took a deep breath. Images of Abraham Lincoln swirled through his head. The apparition was not the former president, but he looked like he could have been from the same era.

"I moved back to the window and looked again," Dylan said. "He was still there, looking out the window with an expressionless face."

Dylan turned and flew down the stairs, heedless of any creaks. He went straight to his dad and woke him up. When he explained what he'd seen, the two of them hurried to the kitchen.

"To my surprise, the light was off and all of the doors and windows were shut and locked as I had left them," Dylan said.

Too shook up to go to bed, Dylan and his dad sat and talked for some time, but they failed to reach any satisfactory conclusions.

Dylan is now married and has moved away, but his parents still live in the house that was built in 1897.

"Our old home has many kind memories, and has always had a warm, good feeling about it," Dylan said. "We've always said that the spirits who spend time there were good people. Sure it's unnerving when doors open or shut with no one there, or when the old eighteenth century clock chimes when it's been broken for over seventy-five years. But we still love our old home and don't mind sharing it with those from the past."

The Weeping Ghost

No one can find the source of the cries.

"Do you know how you go along the rows with the back of your hand to level the books on the shelf?" asked librarian Polly Reber. "Well, I used to work at the Chapman Library, and shortly after I started working there, I would notice this *thunk, thunk, thunk* sound that was just like that. It's a very distinctive sound. When I'd hear it, I'd look around and notice that there was no one else in the building with me."

Polly mentioned the incident to the manager, who told her that many people had heard it. "Some people explained it away as the steam radiators," Polly said. "Others joked that it was the ghost in the building."

But was it a joke? It appears that over the years many have seen or heard some strange things in the Chapman Library, located in Salt Lake City.

One day, a group of neighborhood children came into the library on a Monday, wanting to know why the staff had been dressed in old-fashioned costumes at their library party the day before. They described all the women as wearing long skirts, and the men dressed in black jackets.

But the library was closed on Sunday.

"The kids said there was funny music," said Reber. "It wasn't what they were used to."

The library is situated in a rather transitional neighborhood, settled at different times by cultures as diverse as German, Polynesian, and Vietnamese. "Part of the children who asked about the library party were Caucasian, and part of them were Hispanic," Reber said.

Not all of the ghostly happenings reported at the library have been about fun and games, however. Some of the employees have connected times when there are changes imminent in the library with the sound of a woman crying.

"I used to make deliveries between the different libraries," said Spence Northingham. "One morning I came into Chapman and I could hear a woman crying. So I started going through the building to see if I could help whoever it was, and every time I'd go into a room, it sounded like the crying was coming from the next room. I was sure it was the manager of the branch, and I was worried about what might be wrong. Whoever it was, was crying pretty hard. When I didn't find anyone in the first few rooms, I got so spooked that I quit checking and just got out of there. It was so weird." Two weeks later, the manager was transferred to another branch.

Melanie Walker heard of ghost sightings when she was overseeing the library aides. "I had a lot of aides say that what happened to them is they would walk around a corner and they would see a quick flutter of long skirts go around the end of the stack," Walker said. "I'm not the sort of person who believes in that stuff, so it makes it difficult to hear, but it's happened several times to me. Afterwards, you think, 'Did I really see something, or was it just a shadow?' More than once when someone described seeing something round the corner and the last swirl of the long skirt slipping out of sight, another person would get this horrified look on their face and say, 'I saw that.'"

Most employees and patrons who know about it refer to the ghost as "Annie," because the building was named after Anne Chapman, the first accredited librarian in the

Salt Lake City area. The Chapman Library was built during her lifetime.

"I heard someone crying once," said former employee Dana Smart. "Different people had told me they heard it, but I didn't know if I believed them. One person told me they heard crying when there was talk of closing the library."

Smart's experience in 1993 nearly spelled the closing of the Chapman Branch for good.

"I'd heard the crying a week before. I was going up the stairs and I heard this crying. I thought it was coming from the office we all shared. But no one other than me was there. I had just opened up the building and turned off the alarm.

"Then I had the thought that maybe someone had accidentally been locked in the building all night. I had the feeling that whoever was crying with such heartbreaking sobs had to be in the very next room, so I checked all the rooms, but I didn't find anyone."

A week later, Smart was working an evening shift at the library with a seventeen-year-old library aide named Justin. "There had been a really heavy snowfall and many people were shoveling snow off a lot of roofs," Smart said. "There weren't many people in the building that night. Then Justin said, 'I keep hearing a funny noise.'

"I looked up and just then I heard a loud pop. I had a sneaky hunch that it was the struts breaking in the roof. I cleared half the building and told the patrons they couldn't go to that side of the library.

"As time went on, we heard pops and saw a crack move across the ceiling. I called maintenance and reported the problem, but they weren't too excited about it. The building engineer said he'd have a crew on the roof the next morning to clear off snow. Still concerned, I called the person in charge of the library system that night and requested permission to close early. She said, 'no.'

"Justin and I could see a crack that started in the corner of the ceiling and went beyond the first line of fluorescent lights and was creeping around toward the second set of lights. I was really nervous about it, and even though I was told not to close early, I cleared the building about five or ten minutes before nine o'clock. When I went to get my purse from the office, I had a feeling I should take the money and everything with me, but I didn't. I just got my personal things and walked downstairs with the aide.

"I tried to lock up, but the lower double doors were so sprung from the weight of the snow on the roof that there was too much space between them and the bolts wouldn't go into the floor. I had to settle for just fastening the keyed locks, and then we left.

"Before five the next morning, I got a phone call that the library roof had fallen in."

Could the ghost have been crying about the weakened library? Or could she have been worried about the patrons and staff inside?

Apparently, the ghost of Chapman Library has nothing but people's best interests at heart. According to Smart, "There were a few times when I was sad or upset about something while working at the library, and I had this vague feeling that someone was trying to comfort me. But I never heard or saw anything."

Footsteps on the Stairs

A traumatic death keeps them running for safety.

Back when he was a teenager in Alberta in the early 1900s, Carma Adams' father lived next door to a couple of brothers who were about his same age. The boys often did things together, including ice-skating during the frigid Canadian winters.

One day in the early spring when there was still good skating ice on the deep end of the nearby lake, the boys went out skating as they had numerous times before. For some reason lost in distant memory, Carma's dad missed out on that particular day of skating with his friends.

"The boys went out to ice skate one winter day somewhere in the 1920s, I think," Adams said. "They often skated together, so their parents didn't think anything of it."

When it started getting dark, their parents grew concerned. They sat together in the kitchen, waiting for their sons to return. Their father wondered aloud if he should go out and look for them.

"All of a sudden, they heard the front room door burst open and the sound of two pairs of feet pounding up the stairs. Their mother thought she should go get the boys and fix them some hot chocolate or something, but their dad said it was so late, they must be tired and worn out, especially since they hadn't come into the kitchen looking for food."

That was a little unusual, since the boys were typical perpetually hungry teenagers. The parents finally decided to just let their boys sleep.

In the morning, the boys' mother went upstairs to wake her sons for breakfast. As soon as she stepped inside their room, her heart seized with a sudden dread. She stared at the empty beds, unwilling to believe her eyes. Even though she tried desperately to tell herself that both her sons had just gotten up early and must be elsewhere in the house, she knew with a cold foreboding that their beds hadn't been slept in at all.

With mounting worry, she called out for her husband, who came on the run. He wasted no time in pulling together a search party to find his lost boys, but his worst fears were soon confirmed.

"They eventually found the place in the ice where the boys had broken through and drowned the day before," Adams said.

It was a community tragedy, the loss wringing hearts for weeks afterward.

Their parents missed the boys every day for the rest of their lives. Once they died, the family home passed to others.

But the boys didn't know that.

Anyone who lived in the house from then on would occasionally hear desperate footsteps pounding on the stairs, or even see the boys hurrying up to the second floor and disappear into their bedroom, looking for a place to get warm.

Making the Rounds

Who else watches over the sleeping boys?

Part of Aaron's new job with troubled youth was to take a turn making half-hour checks on the sleeping boys during the graveyard shift. He hadn't been at work long before his coworker, Sandy, told him that the facility used to be a private residence.

"It's only hearsay," Sandy said, "but the story is that a man killed his wife with a gun in the upstairs bedroom. Then he turned the gun on himself."

Earlier, Sandy approached a local doctor who had known both families who had lived in the house. She asked him about the murder/suicide story, but he couldn't offer anything to substantiate it.

Whatever had happened in that house in the past, something mighty strange was going on in the present.

"I don't remember the exact time of night this happened," Sandy said. "My shift was from midnight to eight o'clock AM. We had some boys that got into a little bit of hot water for behaving badly."

When the boys at the home didn't follow certain rules, they had to bring their mattresses down to the living room and sleep on the floor so that the night shift could supervise them closely. On this particular night, there were four or five boys sleeping in the living room. From Sandy's position in the office, she could see straight out to the candy machine set against the living room wall. She was able to hear every rustle and snuffle as the boys in the living room muttered and shifted in their sleep.

Sandy's gaze happened to be fixed on the candy machine when a skinny male with long, straggly hair ran across the living room on silent feet, passing right in front of the machine on his dash across the room.

Sandy shot up from her chair and noticed that the boy on the floor in front of the candy machine stirred in restless sleep.

"Don't be alarmed," Sandy said to her office coworker. Then she headed for the living room to apprehend the errant boy.

Misunderstanding her message, the coworker thought Sandy said "be alarmed," and got up to follow her in case she needed help.

When Sandy stepped into the living room, there was no one to be seen except for the sleeping boys, all on their mattresses where they should be. The restless one calmed and settled into his pillow with a sigh.

Puzzled and concerned, Sandy and her coworker made a check of each boy, searching for signs of feigned sleep, but they couldn't find any. Then they made a thorough circuit of the room, checking every possible hiding place, but the silent running man was nowhere to be found.

Aaron soon discovered that the graveyard shift felt different on some nights than others. He got a sense of when things were right and when they weren't.

"There will be nights when the boys are more restless, and things will kind of creep and move. People will see images—some of the boys will see it too—and they'll be freaked out all night long," Aaron said. "There was one time my flashlight turned itself on."

It was the kind of flashlight with a ring at the neck that twisted, acting as an on/off switch. Aaron set the light face down on a counter, with the handle pointing up into the air. "We were sitting there watching a movie, and all of a sudden, the flashlight turned on." The strange thing is, there was no one near it when it happened.

"One time, a boy said he saw a red hat go across the room. One of the staff jokingly said, 'The red hat, oh, we don't ever talk about the red hat.' Then he walked away. The kid was freaked out," Aaron remembered.

Sandy has heard footsteps coming from the second story, where the infamous murder/suicide bedroom is located. It sounded like someone getting up and walking across the floor. One night it happened three times, but when she or a coworker checked to see who was out of bed when they weren't supposed to be, everyone was asleep and accounted for. "Both my coordinator and I went up three times, and finally we just stood there on the landing, watching, but nothing happened."

In April 2005, Sandy heard one of the boys' radios playing too loudly. Some boys are allowed the privilege of having radios if they've behaved well, but they aren't supposed to exceed a certain volume. Sandy walked over to the offending radio and turned it down. The boy in the bed didn't stir.

The next morning, Sandy had a talk with the boy.

"I knew the radio was too loud," he admitted. "I was going to get up and turn it down, but I saw this guy standing there with his arms folded, looking at me. I was too scared to get up."

The boy was well acquainted with the staff, and he was certain that the person he saw was not one of them.

"Things like that don't spook me out; I don't get scared," Aaron said. "I don't believe spirits can do harm to me, and most ghosts are not out to do bad, they're just people who don't know where they're going."

The Headstone

Two little girls' curiosity disturbed the dead.

Victoria's mother was a seventeen-year-old high school dropout when Victoria was born. "She didn't really want to be a mother," Victoria said. "So most of my childhood was spent at my grandma's house."

Victoria's father often drove to his mother's 1,500 acre farm in Creswell, Oregon, to help out. Every time he did, Victoria went too.

"Grandma was a very happy person, always singing and baking things for people," Victoria said. "She wanted to make people happy. But my own mother was cruel. When I was an infant, she hit my mouth with a spoon until it bled because I wasn't eating the mashed peas she tried to feed me. She didn't really want me. She used to hurt animals too, just because she could. Dad had to make me go home by saying he wouldn't bring me back to Grandma's again if I didn't."

Victoria wanted to live at Grandma's house forever. She was born only two months after her Aunt Connie, Grandma's youngest child, so the two of them were more like sisters. When Victoria grew older, she would often stay at Grandma's house even when her dad went back home. Eventually, when her father realized what his wife was really like, her parents divorced.

Even for the 1970s, Victoria's Grandma was rather old-fashioned. She used a wringer washing machine. The two-story farmhouse had only one bathroom. At one hundred and fifty years old, the house tilted so much that you could put a marble on the high end of the kitchen floor and watch it roll toward the opposite wall, bumping to a sudden stop against the baseboard.

One day, Victoria and Connie went exploring and made a chilling discovery. At the bottom of a hill a little way from the house was an old headstone sticking out of the ground like a decaying tooth. "The date on the tombstone was 1896, and the name on it was Emily," Victoria recalled.

When she asked her father about it, he told her that he and his brother, Kent, had brought the headstone with them when they moved from Canada.

Grandma snorted with amusement. "Why would you bring a headstone from Canada?" she asked. She insisted that it had been there all along, even though Dad was equally insistent that it was one they had brought.

Their curiosity strengthened by the family disagreement, the girls felt drawn to the spot at the bottom of the hill again and again. Every visit made them wonder even more about the origin of the headstone that lay nearly buried in the wild grass. They continued to ask Grandma about it, but didn't get any satisfaction. "We were really curious who was telling the truth," Victoria said. "If Dad really brought it, then there wouldn't be anything under it."

Finally, unsatisfied by the grown-ups' conflicting answers and seeing no other way to get to the bottom of the mystery, the girls agreed on a solution. "One day we just decided to dig it up."

It took them all day long.

"We were around ten or eleven years old," Victoria recalled. "We started digging at about eleven in the morning. It was starting to get dark when we finally hit a wooden box. It was only about three or four feet down."

Their curiosity was suddenly quenched by a bucket of cold fear. The girls dropped their shovels and ran. "We were scared. We went tearing up the hill to the house," Victoria said.

They burst in the door, calling for Grandma so they could tell her she'd been right all along. But they soon discovered they were all alone. Too late, they remembered that Grandma had a meeting at the church that night. She'd already gone, and the church was seventeen miles away.

"We were scared to death," Victoria said. "Grandma's house had old, gross places in the attic that were as scary as heck. In the night, Connie and I were scared to death more than half the time anyway."

It didn't help that a few months earlier, Connie had gone into her room only to see a strange little girl looking through her things. As Connie stared in frank disbelief, the girl faded away. Although Victoria had listened to Connie's tale with rapt attention, Grandma just laughed it off.

"Grandma never got mad," Victoria said. "She made the house cozy. It was always really homey because she made it that way."

But on this particular night, Grandma wasn't home.

"We started watching a TV show called *Night Gallery*, Victoria admitted. "It was about a lady who was in the library and she was locked in with a murderer and they couldn't get out."

It wasn't the best TV show for a couple of girls who were alone and already afraid.

Finally, the two girls turned off the TV and hurried upstairs to snuggle together under the covers in Connie's bed.

There was a draft coming in from one of the bedroom windows. On that windy night, it was enough to push the bedroom door against the doorjamb. Since the house was tilted, the door frame was no longer square, so the door wouldn't fit snugly inside its frame. It bumped against the doorjamb, then swung open. The draft blew the door shut again, and it bounced off the doorframe and swung open again. It was a rhythmic noise, almost comforting in its familiarity.

"All of a sudden, the door stopped swinging," Victoria said. "We peeked out from under our covers and saw a spirit lady standing there holding the door. It was dark, but the light from the moon was coming through the window. She was dressed in old-fashioned clothes, and she wasn't smiling. It looked like we had disturbed her. She had this look on her face of disgust, and we started screaming. We were so scared."

Just in the nick of time, the girls heard the front door of the old house open, followed by the sound of a familiar step on the ground floor.

"As soon as we heard Grandma come in, we screamed, 'Grandma, there's a witch or ghost up here!'

"Grandma said, 'You're being ridiculous.' As soon as she came upstairs, the lady faded."

Victoria and Connie were quick to tell Grandma all about their adventure. Chuckling, she kissed them both and told them to go to sleep.

It seemed as if nothing regarding ghosts or spirits or haunting ever bothered Grandma. If a ghost poked its head into her world, she'd be as likely to offer it some fresh-baked cookies as to scream and run.

"When Grandma was gone, you could feel stuff. But Grandma's spirit was so vibrant and loving that the bad wouldn't stay. When Grandma was there, it didn't feel eerie at all," Victoria remembered.

The girls never went back to fill in the grave. To Victoria's knowledge, nobody did.

Victoria's Grandma is dead and gone, and the house has most likely collapsed by now. Since it rains so much in Oregon, the pile of dirt left beside the old grave by two curious girls has probably slid back into place and filled the old grave back in.

We hope so.

Afterword

Do you believe in ghosts?

It's interesting to note that even among my proofreaders, the jury is out.

Two of my regular proofreaders asked to be excused from reading this manuscript.

A couple of my proofreaders said that this book gave them goose bumps.

One of my proofreaders finished the manuscript, handed it back to me, and said, "I really don't believe in all that stuff."

So, there you have it. From toddlers to grandparents, from demons to angels, these stories were written from interviews I conducted with people who swore that they really happened.

What do you think?

About the Author

Shirley Bahlmann

Shirley Bahlmann is interested in a wide variety of subjects. She started her writing career with the popular *Odds* series of pioneer stories. She has more ideas than she has life left to write them all, but she's determined to get as many written as she can before she moves on to the elusive world of spirits.

Shirley is married to Bob Bahlmann, with whom she's shared the adventure of raising their three oldest sons, Andy, Jeff, and Scott. Now they're in the midst of raising their three youngest boys, Zackary, Brian, and Michael. They claim two beautiful daughters-in-law, Heidi and Jamie, and three exceptional grandchildren, Marcus, Anneke, and Connor.

Feel free to visit Shirley's website at www.shirleybalmann .com to see what she's up to next.

0 26575 79568 4